THE HOURS

THE HOURS:
The Καταρχαί of Hygromanteia
Copyright © 2024 Mat Hadfield
All Rights Reserved.

ISBN 978-1-915933-47-8 (Hardcover)
ISBN 978-1-915933-48-5 (Softcover)

A CIP catalogue for this title is available from the British Library.
10 9 8 7 6 5 4 3 2 1

Except in the case of quotations embedded in critical articles or reviews, no part of this book may be reproduced or transmitted in any form or by any means, electronic or mechanical, including photocopying, recording, or by any information storage and retrieval system, without permission in writing from the publisher.

Mat Hadfield has asserted his moral right to be identified as the author of this work.

Published in 2024
Hadean Press
West Yorkshire
England

www.hadeanpress.com

The Hours

The Καταρχαί of *Hygromanteia*

Mat Hadfield

Reader Endorsements

"Bears and dragons of the stars, the zodiac, the decans, mansions of the moon, spirits, the PGM, Arabic magic, grimoires, all of this and more are found within. This work is extensive in its scope, sources and implications, and has the twin virtues of being both a necessary resource and a valuable guide through the magic of Time and our place within it. Outstanding and essential." – David Rankine, author of *The Grimoire Encyclopaedia*

"This book on the sorceries of the spirits of the hours of the planetary days combines cosmological considerations with eminently practical resources and techniques for a practitioner's own experiments with these potent magics and mysteries of Time itself." – Dr. Alexander Cummins, co-author of *An Excellent Booke Of The Arte Of Magicke*

"A great development of the hemerological material of the Hygromanteia, diligently worked." – Ioannis Marathakis, author of *The Magical Treatise of Solomon, or Hygromanteia*

"Those who delve into this book will be rewarded with a deeper understanding of hemerological concepts that may be used to tap into the mythic cycles at the heart of astrology and magic." – Aequus Nox, podcaster

"Mat Hadfield's *The Hours* is a valuable exegesis of the foundational Hygromanteia, unifying planetary workings, the cyclical nature of the universe, magical timing, spirits of place and more. It provides context, insight, practical experiments and divinatory methods drawing from the Greek magical texts, astral necromancy, the Solomonic stream of occult philosophy and much more. It is indeed a good initiatory text into a deep field of inquiry which will reward the curious reader as well as the practical magician." – Aaman Lamba, author of *The Complete Illustrated Grand Grimoire*

Acknowledgements

Special thanks to all those who have inspired and supported me over the years, especially Jake Stratton-Kent, to whom I am deeply indebted for his pioneering work, and to Ioannis Marathakis for his critical edition of *The Magical Treatise of Solomon or Hygromanteia*. I would also like to express my deep gratitude to David Rankine, Stephen Skinner, Joseph H. Peterson, Dr Alexander Cummins, Brian Johnson, Eric Perdue, Aaman Lamba, and Kadmus for their passion and dedication to our field of study and practice. My thanks also go to Dis Carr, Aequus Nox and Jae Cro for being my confidants and collaborators, o Simôné Karlson for their eagle eyes, and to both Erzebet Barthold and Matt Moreash for believing in me and being fantastic editors.

Finally, I'd like to thank my wife for her unwavering love.

"Time is the substance I am made of. Time is a river which sweeps me along, but I am the river; it is a tiger which destroys me, but I am the tiger; it is a fire which consumes me, but I am the fire."
Jorge Luis Borges, *Labyrinths: Selected Stories & Other Writings*

Now [the God's name] is [composed of] nine Names, in advance of which you should say, with the [prayer on the] stele, [those of] the Gods of the Hours and of the Days [and] those set over the weeks, and the compulsive formula for these. For without these the God will not listen, but, thinking you uninitiated, will refuse to receive [you], unless you emphatically say to him the Names of the Lord of the Day and of the Hour [...]
For without these you can accomplish nothing of the things you find written in the Key.
PGM XIII. 424-432
The Eighth Book of Moses
139(?)-400 CE

Yours is the eternal processional way in which your seven-lettered name is established for the harmony of the Seven sounds of the Planets which utter their voices according to the Twenty-Eight forms of the Moon,

SAR APHARA APHARA I ABRAARM ARAPHA ABRAACH PERTAŌMĒCH AKMĒCH IAŌ OYE Ē IAŌ OYE EIOY AEŌ EĒOY IAŌ

CONTENTS

Definitions . . . xi
Introduction . . . 1
Part I: Beginnings
    Inaugurations . . . 3
    Hygromanteia . . . 7
    The Manuscripts . . . 8

Part II: Context
    The North Star . . . 9
    Four Kings . . . 19
    The Aerial Spirits . . . 21
    Thwarting Angels . . . 25

Part III: Theory
    Determining the Hours . . . 28
    Friendship and Enmity . . . 30
    The Dignitaries and Virtues of the Planets . . . 35
    DIS-ASTER . . . 37
    The 12 Signs of the Zodiac and their Virtues . . . 39

Part IV: Lunar Hemerology
    Concerning the Dragon who resides in the Ninth Heaven . . . 43
    The Beneficial Days of the Moon . . . 44
    Concerning the Lunar Observations of the Persian Philosopher Zanates . . . 47
    The Beneficial & Malign Days of the Month . . . 51

Part V: The Catalogue
    The Names of the Hours and their Offices . . . 52
    Notes on the Days . . . 66
    Seven Hours of Saturn and the Sorcery of the *Hygromanteia* . . . 87

Part VI: The Instruction
    Apotropaia . . . 89
    An Alternative Rubric for the Harvesting of Materia . . . 91
    An Opening Rite . . . 92

A Ritual to Selene . . . 97
The First Spirits of Day and Night . . . 100

Part VII: The Gods of Time
Images, Prayers, and Conjurations . . . 102
Address to Aion . . . 112
A Spell of the Bear which Accomplishes Anything . . . 114

Appendix: Satanael . . . 120

Bibliography . . . 125

Index . . . 129

Definitions

Καταρχαί, Greek. Katarchai: 'Inaugurations' of activity. Initiatives, Beginnings – used to determine the best time to start a particular action, both mundane and magical. For more information see Alexander Jones, 'Astrologers and Their Astronomy', In *Oxyrhynchus: A City and its Texts*, ed. by A. K Bowman et. al. (London: The Egypt Exploration Society, 2007) 307-314, and Johannes Thomann, 'From *katarchai* to *ikhtiyārāt*: The Emergence of a New Arabic Document Type Combining Ephemerides and Almanacs', in *Proceedings of the 28th International Congress of Papyrology Barcelona 2016*, ed. by Alberto Nodar, Sofía Torallas Tovar, et. al., (Barcelona: Publications de l'Abadia de Montserrat, 2019) 342-354.).

Hemerology, English: *"A method of divination that is common to civilizations worldwide, links the outcome of events to the occult nature of the times at which these events occur. Specific units of time, such as seasons, months, days, or hours, were thought to have hidden, intrinsically auspicious or inauspicious qualities that influenced the outcome of actions undertaken and events taking place during these periods."* From Lászlo Sándor Chardonnens, 'Hemerology in Medieval Europe', in *Books of Fate and Popular Culture in Early China: The Daybook Manuscripts of the Warring States, Qin, and Han*, ed. by Donald Harper and Mark Kalinowski (Leiden: Brill, 2017) 373-407 (p. 373).

From Ancient Greek ἡμέρᾱ (*hēmérā*, day; date)… + *-ology* (from Ancient Greek -λογίᾱ (*-logíā*, *"suffix indicating the study of something, or a branch of knowledge"*)… From <https://en.wiktionary.org/wiki/hemerology>.

Ἥλιος

Come, come to me from the Four Winds of the World, O air-traversing great God.
Hear me in every ritual which I perform, and grant my desires completely,
for I, your prophet, know your Signs, Symbols and Forms,
I know who you are each Hour and I know your twelve holy Names

PHARAKOUNĒTH, SOUPHI, AMEKRANEBECHEO
THŌYTH, SENTHENIPS, ENPHANCHOUPH, BAI SOLBAI,
OUMESTHŌTH, DIATIPHĒ, PHĒOUS PHŌOUTH, BESBYKI,
MOU RŌPH, AERTHOĒ

Cat, Dog, Serpent, Scarab, Donkey, Lion,
Goat, Bull, Falcon, Baboon, Ibis, Crocodile

Come now, swiftly, for I have spoken your Names and Symbols,
Come to me in your holy circuit of the holy Spirit,
O Founder, O God of Gods, Lord of the World,
You who have divided by your own divine Spirit
The Universe; first from the firstborn you appeared,
Created carefully from the Abyssal Waters of Nun,
O you who founded the Worlds:
Abyss, Earth, Fire, Water, Air, and in turn
Ether and roaring rivers, red-faced Moon,
Heaven's Stars, Morning Stars, and the Whirling Wanderers.
By your council do they attend us in this Hour

Come swiftly and hear these Words

Introduction

It is clear, from what survives from Antiquity up until the largely corrupted expressions of systems of magical Time found in the European grimoires, that there are structures inherent to the cyclic expressions of the Universe that determine certain modalities of interaction between the sorcerer and the World, and that these structures have been explored many times over throughout history in countless cultures. These are often expressed as the Names of Spirits, Names which, when called upon during appropriate astrologically significant moments of Time, confine and orchestrate specific permutations of the virtues of the sublunar realm. In their steady march these Names provide a temporal map of sequential gates through which certain sorcerous actions find avenues of expression and reification. Through their waxing and waning we find ourselves deeply embedded within an ecology of which we are but a single node within an infinite web of interdependence. Approaching in this manner, we come to consider Time as an object, not simply as an artificial and abstract concept defined by the progress of ticking hands upon the surface of a clock, but something through which we are intimately interconnected, to which we are bound and subject, and within which we are interwoven as part of the natural world along with the rising of the Sun, the phases of the Moon, and our own tides and seasons. This Time is non-linear, cyclic, eternal, and mythic.

The Guardians of these thresholds which blossom, flower, and wilt forth from this unending flow provide points of access through which we are able to reach out and negotiate with the Universe. We find that Time is as possessed of Spirit as any Location and, knowing the Names which resonate with coherence within this river, we are granted the sight to engage in its cartography. It may even be better to say that knowing our position in Time allows us to access what is known as *Mythic Location*, whereby the sorcerer casts their spell at the precise moment alongside all those who came before them. Our own voice is added to the choir, making our call as much an act of necromancy as it is a conjuration of the *moment*. We are there, at dawn under a waxing crescent Moon, materia to hand, secret Names upon our lips, with the voices of centuries past joining our own.

Time breathes, inhaling and exhaling as a great beast, pulsing as a beating heart in intricate cycles that loop and spin through ceaseless eternity. With this knowledge, the sorcerer finds themselves in possession of a *Key*, able to marry and weave the fluidity of Location within Time, to move through the liminal Space between Night and Day, and to stand firm at the Crossroads of the Worlds.

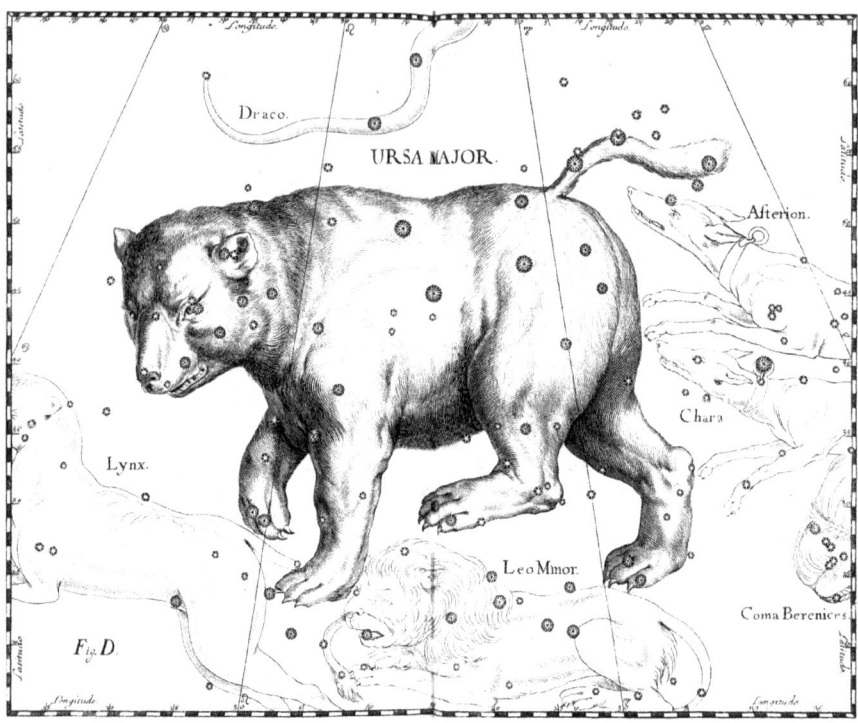

FIG.1: JOHANNIS HEVELII (1611–1687), PRODROMUS ASTRONOMIAE.

PART I: Beginnings

✠

Inaugurations

Time, the Spirits which reside within its flow, and their conjuration during ritual are important aspects of the continued reconstruction of not only the grimoire tradition, but also of the magic which stems from the Ancient World. Many earlier European grimoires, those being from roughly the twelfth to the sixteenth century, possess the Names of the Hours, Days, and Seasons which can trace their source to *Liber Razielis* Book VI, 'Liber Temporum'.[1] These include the highly influential *Munich Manual* (CLM 849)[2] which was the source for texts of the *Lucidarium artis Nigromanticę*; Ghent 1021A, VSG334, and VRL 1115;[3] *The Keys of Rabbi Solomon* found in Wellcome MS 4670;[4] and perhaps most famously, the *Heptameron* of the *Fourth Book of Occult Philosophy*[5] by pseudo-Agrippa. Another source of the Names or titles of Spirits which represent the permutations of the Planets, Zodiac, and the Seasons can be found in the *Summa Sacre Magice*. By the time we reach the tail-end of the seventeenth century, most of these timings have been lost, streamlined, redacted, or are only mentioned in instructional procedures such as the astrological conditions necessary for the creation of talismans or magical tools. We do see more examples of the use of magical timing in spells, especially concerning the handling of certain materia magica, but often without any explanation as to why these Hours bear any importance. As a result of this, many practitioners today struggle to understand their necessity.

Thomann describes the use of magical timing for beginning certain actions as such:

---

1 Rome, Vatican Library, MS Vat. Reg. lat. 1300, fols 45, 61.

2 Richard Kieckhefer, *Forbidden Rites* (University Park: Penn State Press, 1997) pp. 181-3.

3 Joseph H. Peterson, *Elucidation of Necromancy* (Fort Worth: Ibis Press 2021) pp. 139-142.

4 Stephen Skinner and David Rankine, *The Veritable Key of Solomon* (Singapore: Golden Hoard Press, 2010) p. 103.

5 Pseudo-Agrippa, *The Fourth Book of Occult Philosophy*, ed. by Stephen Skinner, trans. by Robert Turner (Fort Worth: Ibis Press, 2015) pp. 61-63.

Hemerology looks back upon a long tradition in the Eastern Mediterranean region. Lists of lucky and unlucky days exist from the second millennium BCE onwards. A Hieratic papyrus found in Lahun is the earliest such list. It is a calendar in which each day is either labelled as good (nefer) in black, or as bad (dju) in red, and three days are labelled as both good and bad. Hemerology was widespread. A Linear B document is the first example in the Greek language. In the Greek and Roman world, hemerology was already well-established at an early date. But these practices were based on cultic or civil calendars. In Hellenistic Egypt, a new system of astrological interpretation of planetary constellations arose, first in the form of horoscopic astrology, based on the moment of birth of an individual, later, in the 1st century BCE, in a new continuous form of astrology, the καταρχαί. The first Greek author known to have written on the subject was Dorotheos of Sidon (50-100 CE). The Greek text is lost, but an Arabic translation survived. The καταρχαί, literally the 'beginnings', were used to determine the best time to start a particular action.[6]

We find then that the manuscripts of the *Hygromanteia* were repositories of sorcerous hemerological knowledge, detailing the Names of Spirits which preside over the Hours of the Days of the week, the materia they were associated with, their offices and the methods whereby they may be conjured. With this knowledge the karcist or sorcerer-priest was able to make the best use of the καταρχαί detailed within to create magical objects which possessed the virtues of the Gods and Spirits which cohere with the various permutations of the wandering stars and particularly the Moon.

What makes these techniques of particular interest and value is that they represent one of several bridges that exist between the venerable Greek Magical Papyri (PGM)[7] and the grimoires of the Mediterranean and later northern Europe. Summarising the work of Torijano[8] in their *Veritable Key of Solomon*, Skinner and Rankine state that,

---

6 Thomann, p. 342.

7 Hans Dieter Betz, *The Greek Magical Papyri in Translation*, 2nd edition, (Chicago: University of Chicago Press, 1996).

8 Pablo A. Torijano, *Solomon the Esoteric King: From King to Magus, Development of a Tradition* (Leiden: Brill, 2002).

He postulates the entry of (*Hygromanteia*) into Europe through southern Italy in the sixth century CE. As this was one of the strongholds of the Byzantine Empire, it would help to explain the earliest *Key of Solomon* being found in Italian. This early date is also supported by the similarities between the material found in the *Hygromanteia* and the *Greek Magical Papyri*, such as the Collapse of Solomon, with the technique of divination using a pure boy as a medium. It is also supported by finding the *Testament of Solomon* bound up with several of the manuscript copies of the *Hygromanteia*.[9]

This goes some way in explaining the inclusion of the Name *Loutzepher* as the chief demon of Wednesday, a Latin title in its Italian pronunciation which simply wouldn't have been used by the Greeks of the Middle Ages, "since the Greek equivalent, *Eōsphoros*, had been long established through the Septuagint tradition of the Old Testament, the Patristic literature and the liturgical language."[10] Of course, there are several other competing arguments, one of which supports a Cretan origin in the thirteenth or fourteenth century when Crete was under Venetian rule, which many believe to be more likely given the tolerance of the era and Crete's long history of occult lore.[11]

It is likely after the transmission of *Hygromanteia* into Europe that we see the beginning of hierarchical transformations concerning the four rulers of the Directions. These Spirits always possess the highest authority over collections of Spirits and it may be best to instead describe them as 'directing spirits' in that they behave as shepherds who reside within the four regions of the World. These leading Spirits, namely *Loutzipher*, *Berzeboul*, *Astarōth*, and *Asmodai*, rule over the East, South, West, and North respectively and play an important role within the hierarchical structure of *Hygromanteia*, forming the leading force of the internal hierarchy responsible for the more Infernal forms of magic found within the manuscripts. Unlike the later European grimoires, however, we don't find catalogues of Demons alongside their descriptions, offices, and sigils. All of these aspects of the more familiar forms of Solomonic magic evolve later after cross-pollination with and innovation from other cultures.

---

9 Skinner and Rankine, p. 62.

10 Ioannis Marathakis, *The Magical Treatise of Solomon or Hygromanteia*, (Singapore: Golden Hoard Press, 2011) p. 75.

11 Marathakis, p. 75.

The Directions are in many ways connected to the Winds, although there remain many differences from the Classical Greek conceptualisation of the *Anemoi*. In the Christian traditions these Winds are seen as being 'Unclean', an evolution which coincides with the earlier neutral meaning of the Greek *daimon* becoming the infernal Christian *demon*. There is also a potentially lost or long-sublimated astrological component inherent to the directions, given the sheer abundance of astrological considerations within the manuscripts of *Hygromanteia* as well as the rich stellar lore found within the Greek Magical Papyri, the most important of which involves the thirty-six Egyptian decans and the heliacal rising of Sirius in the Sign of Cancer which initiates the flooding of the Nile and marked the beginning of the Egyptian new year. Stratton-Kent writes,

> Simplistically speaking the decans would rise with the Sun for ten days each year until the reappearance of Sothis, the first and last. As the cycle continued the decans progressed to the West they descended into the underworld, not to reappear for 70 days. There is wide agreement that they are the origin of the 24 hour clock, and also of planetary hours. At the time of the heliacal rising of Sothis in the summer twelve decans rose before dawn. Ten hours of daylight, to which were added an hour of twilight at either end of the day.[12]

What's more, we find rich descriptions of the hours in the Egyptian Book of Gates, a cosmological treatise dating to the New Kingdom period[13] which describes the architecture and inhabitants of the Tuat, the Underworld through which the Sun God, Ra traverses for twelve hours each night.[14] This ancient text details the necessary passwords for the chthonic guardians which reside within this cyclic, eschatological time, the conclusion of which is the end of the deceased soul's journey through the Underworld and the rebirth of the Sun.

---

12 Jake Stratton-Kent, *The Testament of Cyprian the Mage* (London: Scarlet Imprint, 2014) p. 160.

13 16th century BCE and the 11th century BCE

14 E. A. Wallis Budge, *The Egyptian Heaven and Hell*. London. 1905.

Hygromanteia

The *Hygromanteia* is a collection of Greek-language manuscripts of Byzantine origin, many of which date to the fourteenth and fifteenth-century of the common era; however, there is significant consensus that its antecedents can be traced back to the sixth century CE. These texts utilise magical techniques and processes which can be traced back even further through the Greek Magical Papyri and further still into the archaic past. *Hygromanteia* (Ὑγρομαντεία) is a Greek word which translates to 'Water bowl divination', much as *Nekromanteia* means divination via the Dead. This is not the text group's historical name, which is more likely something to the effect of 'The Magical Treatise of Solomon', or 'The Instruction of Solomon'. The primary source document for the Names of the Hours upon which the current text is based, MS Monacensis Gr. 70, bears the verbose title, *The Little Key of the Entire Art of Hygromanteia, discovered by various authors and composed by Solomon, in which he seems to write to his son, Rehoboam.* Of all the manuscripts extant, only two, MS Monacensis Gr. 70 and MS Athonicus Dion. 282, bear the word *Hygromanteia* in their title. The definition of this word is also somewhat debatable, and as with the titles of this text group, is the result of a series of redactions throughout its history. Examples of water bowl divination do appear within several versions of the manuscript, but the focus throughout is more often the description of astrological hemerology and talismanic-image magic. Marathakis writes, "According to them [Skinner and Rankine], the word Hygromanteia does not mean water divination in this context, but applies to the ancient practice of constraining demons in hydriai, that is to say, urns, water jars or metallic water vessels."[15] While not definitive, this definition appears far more suitable while also placing these manuscripts in relation to the archæological evidence of the practice of conjuring or trapping demonic Spirits within vessels of water, a practice which spans the history of the ancient Near and Middle East, North Africa, and the Mediterranean.

---

15 Marathakis, p. 35.

✠
The Manuscripts

Having access to Marathakis' text: *The Magical Treatise of Solomon, or Hygromanteia*, as well as Greenfield's *Traditions of Belief*, will make understanding the following far easier and also allow the reader to take my proposed suggestions and form their own opinions when necessary. There are several instances where forming a concrete solution was essentially impossible given the ambiguity of the extant textual evidence.

Marathakis lists nineteen separate manuscripts, whereas the following analysis was taken from a comparative study of only five of the most relevant to our subject, all of which contain catalogues of the Names of the Hours. These include MS Harleianus 5596 (H), MS Atheniensis 1265 (A), MS Gennadianus 45 (G), MS Monacensis Gr. 70 (M), and MS Bernardaceus (B). Other manuscripts are detailed as they become relevant to the study. While H, A, G, and B are primarily used as comparative texts, Monacensis was chosen as the base catalogue from which to attempt this reconstruction. Both H and A have large numbers of lacunae, making them unsuitable as a base. Ultimately M was chosen over G due to some minor lacunae and complications that don't affect M. B was often useful as a means to see where errors had crept in, but is largely unusable due to its high level of comparative corruption.

As for the Offices of each Hour, these were collated from H, M, and G. There are many issues with H, although it has some interesting variations which helped produce a more complete list despite the number of copy errors and lacunae. M and G are, for the most part, in agreement about the majority of their entries, with some notable differences which add dimension to each office. An example is the Ninth Hour of Day on Tuesday: M states, 'For taking loot from a castle', whereas G states, 'for conquering the whole castle'. A minor distinction, and yet overall it fleshes out the general meaning of conquering and plundering the bastion of one's enemies. In contrast, for the very same Hour H states, 'Do whatever you want'. When we observe the virtues at play we see the Solar forces being projected through the prism of Mars, a solar-martial combination which allows for the overthrowing of authority.

Part II: Context

✠

The North Star

*Silence! Silence!
I am a Star, wandering about with you, and shining forth from the deep*[16]

The North and its Winds are often connected with malefic and often necromantic practices. As the Sun sets in the West and the night sky comes to life in the darkness, we look to this region of the Sky confident in our knowledge of the stars we will find. The ability to find the Pole star among the inhabitants of the northern hemisphere enabled our ancestors to orient themselves in Space, and recognising and understanding the movement of the constellations which surround it enabled them to orient themselves equally in Time, as their relative positions reveal the season we find ourselves within. This is a complex subject and so perhaps we should begin by explaining why we as karcists, magicians, and sorcerers should care about this often-maligned region of the sky in the first place.

With the advent of modernity, humanity has, for the most part, been separated from our connection to the beating heart of the World, the pulse of which is the vital essence of what we call *magic*. To save ourselves from the fear of the night we have drowned out the light of the Stars, we have lost our knowledge of their patterns and forgotten their stories. I don't mean to romanticise the past, but I will lament the present. Our relationship with the World is deeply symbiotic; we are a product of its chemistry and aeons of time, intrinsically interwoven, not only with the soil of this small blue orb, but fundamentally with the very stars themselves. The calcium in our bones, the iron in our blood—all of it came from the deaths of great stars many billions of years ago. We are creatures born from vast processes of roiling chaos, order, and time, and given our current understanding of the universe, there is nothing mundane about our existence.

Part of returning to a deeper understanding of the universe surrounding us involves recognising our location within it, and this can most readily be done by observing the World instead of siloing ourselves away from it. This also involves adopting a magical hermeneutic, which

---

16 'The Mithras Liturgy' of PGM IV. 475-829. See Betz, p. 49.

isn't to say that we dispense with the rational or the scientific, but instead that we allow one to inform the other, and most of all begin a process of engagement which substantiates both, much in the same way in which colour theory, chemistry, and culture influenced the development of Art. The movement of the Sun then, is our first observation, it rises in the East, bringing light and warmth, its power fresh and new. It ascends to its height in the sky, then descends toward the opposite horizon. Finally it is gone for a time, and we are surrounded by the pinprick light of its distant cousins. By entering into the mythic, we see the Sun born each day, rise to power, then fade and weaken, before the host of stars emerge to take its place, and just as our local Star has its movements and stories, so do they. We also come to be familiar with the motions of the Moon, her phases of light and darkness, waxing and waning as she moves across the sky. Looking beyond Her we observe that the Stars behind shift as the year progresses, a small number of them move rapidly, some over days, others over many years These are the Wanderers, which today we call the Planets.

There is however, among all this swirling, a region of the sky that remains to the human eye fixed and motionless. It is the axial pole around which everything else is animated. This is the North Star, and it remains in this place over generations, unmoved and eternal. Our grandparents knew it, and so did theirs, and so on. But there was a time, a very long time ago, before the current Age, when this Pole Star was not located in this position, and that period of history has since been subsumed into the myth and stories of the heavens and the night sky. We learn in awe and maybe even a little fear, that the North Star of old was usurped by the one who stands there today. This process takes thousands of years, and as it occurs cultures and stories are forced to change; the Gods are overthrown.

This region of the night sky has been neglected almost entirely by modern occulture, and information about its importance has been mostly lost to history. There remain enough scraps and fragments of evidence however that we can attempt some form of reconstruction. There are both mythological and magical connections to ancient, sinister, and often malevolent attributions related to the northern constellation Ursa Major[17] which have come to prominence through the gradual precession of Earth's rotational axis and changing or usurping of the Pole Star; one such multicultural myth being the motif of the slaying of a great dragon. A potential origin of this motif may have been the shift of the designation of

---

17 Particularly with the Egyptian Set, although this God was not always considered to have an evil connotation.

Pole Star from *Thuban* (α Draconis), the brightest Star in the constellation of Draco, to *Polaris* (α *Ursae Minoris*) in the constellation of Ursa Minor. Ursa Major circles around both constellations of Draco and Ursa Minor, with the Pole star at the centre of this complex, the axis-mundi, being the point which connects the Earth to both the Celestial and the Underworld. While both Ursa Major and Minor are each composed of seven primary stars, Ursa Major is associated with the Bear, while Ursa Minor, or *Little Bear*, was imagined by the Egyptians as a Bull. The number seven has such a vast importance to the nature of magic and is intimately connected with our present topic of these Stars. We find it is also of great significance to the Greek language itself, which possesses seven vowel sounds, as well as being the number of the visible Planets, the Seven Hathors and Sisters of the Pleiades cluster.[18] For Christians the number seven remains an important, albeit cryptic number, being one of the primary values mentioned throughout Revelation.[19] Going back in history further we find the Mesopotamian myth of Inanna, who descended into the Underworld through seven Gates before reaching the throne room of her sister, Ereshkigal, and the seven Anunnaki, or Judges. The importance of this number simply cannot be taken lightly and has had a profound impact upon religion and magic throughout history.

Collectively the three constellations of Draco and Ursa Major and Minor never set below the horizon, and examples of their *undying* nature can be found in various examples from the Greek Magical Papyri. The overthrowing of the Pole star from Thuban to Polaris was a very gradual event, taking around three-and-half thousand years, between 3000 BCE and 500 CE, and it is safe to assume that these shifts in the night sky must have had a significant impact on culture, religion, and magic. Between

---

18 Amelia Sparavigna, 'The Pleiades: the celestial herd of ancient timekeepers', ArXiv.org>physics (2008) <arXiv:0810.1592v1> notes, "The Seven Hathors of the Celestial Herd were named in a spell of the Book of the Dead and these names are: the 'Lady of the Universe', the 'Skystorm', 'The hidden one, presiding over her place', 'You, from Khemmis', the 'Red Hair', the 'Bright Red' and 'Your Name prevails over the West'. Often accompanied by Osiris-Apis, Bull of the West, and the oars representing the four cardinal points, in the vignettes enclosed to the text in the 'Book of the Dead', the seven cows and the bull are depicted in front of the offering tables of worshippers. The representation of animals (wild or domesticated) in front of an offering pole or table is also common in the Indus Valley civilization."

19 For example, Revelation 5.6 (King James Version): "And I beheld, and, lo, in the midst of the throne and of the four beasts, and in the midst of the elders, stood a Lamb as it had been slain, having seven horns and seven eyes, which are the seven Spirits of God sent forth into all the earth."

these dates we find the stars Kochab and Pherkad, otherwise known as Beta and Gamma Ursae Minoris, held the loose role of Twin Pole stars from around 1700 BCE to 300 CE, although they were never truly close enough to be considered officially recognised as such in Antiquity. The Greek explorer Pytheas of Massalia (350-306 BCE) described this region as being devoid of stars.[20]

Examining one of the Bear Spells, a necromantic bowl divination addressed to Typhon found in PGM IV. 154-285, we discover a description of this Titan in relation to the Pole Star, specifically in lines 190-191, "I am He who closed heaven's double gates and put to sleep the serpent which must not be seen", referring to the northern constellation of Draco in relation to the *Gate of Death* in Cancer, through which souls pass into the Underworld, and the *Gate of the Gods* in Capricorn, the entrance point for souls seeking incarnation. These Gates form a "critical polarity in the sideral eschatology from Egyptian and Chaldean traditions."[21] Lines 263 to 265 of the same spell read:

> I call you who did first control gods' wrath,
> You who are the midpoint of the stars above,
> You, master Typhon, you I call, who are
> The dreaded sovereign o'er the firmament.[22]

This highlights the Northern quality of Typhon, who is identified here in the midpoint of the night sky and who alongside Set, with whom he is syncretised in Hellenic Egypt, is associated with the seven stars of Ursa Major and the serpentine qualities of the constellation Draco; sovereign over the firmament and yet also possessing a deeply telluric or chthonic nature which places the Underworld, indeed even Tartarus, in this celestial location.

Later in lines 663–704 of PGM IV. 475–829, a section of what is commonly known as the *Mithras Liturgy*, but which is better referred to as *The Mysteries of Helios-Mithras*, we find this remarkable passage [emphasis mine]:

---

20 Pytheas of Massalia, was the first known early scientific explorer to experience the theorised perpetual day of the northern polar reaches, known as the midnight sun. See Philip G. Kaplan, 'Pytheas of Massalia' in *The Encyclopedia of Ancient History*, ed. by. Roger S. Bagnall (Malden: Wiley-Blackwell, 2012).
21 Stratton-Kent, *The Testament of Cyprian the Mage*, Book I, p. 172.
22 Betz, p. 43.

After saying this, you will see the doors of Heaven thrown open, and **seven** virgins coming from deep within, dressed in linen garments, and with the faces of **asps**. They are called the Fates of heaven and wield golden wands. When you see them, greet them in this manner:

Hail, O **seven** Fates of Heaven, O noble and good virgins,
O sacred ones and companions of **MINIMIRROPHOR**,
O most holy guardians of the **four pillars**! Hail to you,
the first, **CHREPSENTHAĒS**! Hail to you, the second,
MENESCHEĒS! Hail to you, the third, **MECHRAN**! Hail
to you, the fourth, **ARARMACHES**! Hail to you, the fifth,
ECHOMMIĒ! Hail to you, the sixth, **TICHNONDAĒS**! Hail
to you, the seventh, **EROU ROMBRIĒS**!

There also come forth another **seven gods**, who have the faces of black bulls, in linen loincloths, and in possession of **seven golden diadems**. They are the so-called **Pole Lords of heaven**, whom you must greet in the same manner, each of them with his own name:

Hail, O guardians of the **pivot**, O sacred and brave youths, who turn at one command **the revolving axis of the vault of heaven**, who send out thunder and lightning and jolts of earthquakes and thunderbolts against the nations of impious people, but to me, who am pious and god-fearing, you send health and soundness of body and acuteness of hearing and seeing, and calmness in the present **good hours** of this day, O my lords and powerfully ruling gods!

Hail to you, the first, **AIERŌNTHI**! Hail to you, the
second, **MERCHBIMEROS**! Hail to you, the third,
ACHRICHIOUR! I Hail to you, the fourth, **MESARGILTŌ**!
Hail to you, the fifth, **CHICHRŌALITHO**! Hail to you,
the sixth, **ERMICHTHATHŌPS**! Hail to you, the seventh,
EORASICHĒ!

Now when they take their place, here and there, in order, look in the **air** and you will see lightning bolts going down, and lights flashing, and the earth shaking, and a God descending, a God immensely great, having a bright appearance, youthful, golden-haired, with a white tunic and a golden crown and trousers, and holding in his right hand a golden shoulder of a young **bull: this is the Bear which moves and turns heaven around, moving upward and downward in accordance with the hour**. Then you will see lightning bolts leaping from his eyes and stars from his body. [23]

This not only describes the God Names of the seven Guardian rulers of the serpent-faced virgins of Ursa Major as well as the bull-faced lords of Ursa Minor, but also quite specifically outlines the importance of this region of the sky while also specifying the Bear, Ursa Major, as the driving, turning, or motivating force which animates the stars *in accordance with the hour*. What matters most of all about these stars is that they are immortal, never setting below the horizon, and it is this immortality which the sorcerer is attempting to acquire for the duration of the ritual (lines 475-485 of PGM IV. 475-829) by gaining access to this celestial-chthonic region. The God encountered in this mytho-location, of "a bright appearance, youthful, golden-haired, with a white tunic and a golden crown and trousers, and holding in his right hand a golden shoulder of a young bull," [24] is not the above-mentioned Typhon, but Helios-Mithras. While both of these Gods may seem far removed, they are arguably located in this celestial region due to their centrality to their respective cosmogenic myths. The technique itself appears to have been considered useful and highly adaptable by the author of PGM IV and is shared by many other authors in the same era, most notably within PGM XIII, the *Eighth Book of Moses*.

We find other examples within the PGM and the *Leyden Papyrus* where Ursa Major often goes by the name, 'foreleg', where the constellation is first located within the sky and deliberately positioned behind the sorcerer-priest during 'god arrival' rites. Two such examples are described within PDM xiv. 117-49 and PDM xiv. 232-38. Both of these texts, written in Demotic, include instructions to perform certain ritual actions seven times, a common enough instruction throughout the Greek Magical Papyri but which is here clearly connected via sympathy to the Seven Stars of Ursa Major.

If we bring our focus now to the beginning of the grimoire tradition, we find the North is the home of the great Spirit of lust and wrath,

---

23 Betz, pp. 51-52.
24 Betz, p. 52.

Asmodeus.²⁵ This Spirit King is also highly connected to the number seven, murdering Sarah's seven husbands in the second to third century CE Book of Tobit, and bearing serpentine iconography and heraldry in his various descriptions throughout the grimoires. He is also given the name 'Demon of Wrath', further underscoring his Northern quality as we have seen from the excerpt from line 236 of PGM IV above. Arguably his first appearance within the tradition of Solomonic Magic is found within the *Testament of Solomon*, where in verse 21 he declares to the King:

> But how shall I answer thee, for thou art a son of man; whereas I was born an angel's seed by a daughter of man, so that no word of our heavenly kind addressed to the earth-born can be overweening. **Wherefore also my star is bright in heaven, and men call it, some the Wain, and some the dragon's child. I keep near unto this star.** So ask me not many things; for thy kingdom also after a little time is to be disrupted, and thy glory is but for a season. And short will be thy tyranny over us; and then we shall again have free range over mankind, so as that they shall revere us as if we were gods, not knowing, men that they are, the names of the angels set over us.²⁶

While the Homeric *Bear* of Ursa Major is common today, the *Wain* or wagon has its origin in Mesopotamia and persists in the German *Großer Wagen*, or 'Greater Wagon', while in Ireland and the UK it often goes by the 'Plough'. Ursa Minor was also referred to as the 'Wain of Heaven' by both the Babylonians and the Phoenicians, which initially led to some confusion as to which constellation Asmodeus was referring to, as the current home of the Pole Star is Ursa *Minor*, the Bull of Egyptian astrology. This confusion isn't helped as both constellations are referred to as a *wain* and both possess seven prominent Stars.

---

25 One of the oldest Spirits of the grimoire tradition, making appearances throughout the Zoroastrian Avesta (The Gathas), the Quran (Surah 38:34), Biblical Apocrypha (The Book of Tobit), and an extensive range of manuscripts found in the grimoire tradition. There is some suggestion of this Spirit dating back to ancient Persia via the Name's potential etymological connection to Aēšma-Daēva (𐬀𐬉𐬱𐬨𐬀⸱𐬛𐬀𐬉𐬎𐬎𐬀*/ *aēṣmadaēuua), Wrath-Demon, although this is contested.

26 F. C. Conybeare, trans., 'The Testament of Solomon', *Jewish Quarterly Review*, 11 (October 1898), 1-45 (p. 20).

As we shall see, Asmodeus, or *Asmodai*, is found throughout the *Hygromanteia* as the King of the Northern Quarter[27] and is linked to the planet Saturn, which is intimately connected with both Time and the Ninth Heaven, which resides above the Fixed Stars. In Agrippa's 'Geomancy', found in the *Fourth Book of Occult Philosophy*, we find Hasmodai or Chasmodai as the ruler of the Moon and Cancer and the two geomantic symbols Populus and Via.[28] Jake Stratton-Kent also connects this Spirit to the Intelligence of the Intelligence of the Moon[29] found in the Agrippa's Planetary Squares, while in *A Book of the Offices of Spirits* and the later *Ars Goetia* of the *Lesser Key of Solomon* we find Asmoday under the aegis of Amaymon, who reigns in Capricorn in which Saturn finds himself domicile. In this form we find this Spirit described as bearing a serpent's tail and riding upon an infernal dragon.

When we examine the Decans, we find that Cancer's three divisions are attributed to Venus, Mercury, and the Moon, while Capricorn's divisions go to Jupiter, Mars, and the Sun, respectively. The missing Planetary attribution in this celestial axis is thus Saturn, about which both constellations orbit in the North. Finally, according to Agrippa, Taurus, the Bull, in which the Moon is exalted, is ruled by the Angelic form of this Spirit, Asmodel or Ashmodiel. This Sign possesses Decans attributed to Mercury, as well as both the Moon and Saturn. In the 9th Key[30] of Harley 6482, which is attributed to the Moon, we find a description[31] of this Saturnian Decan described as a "figure riding upon a **Dragon** with **seven** heads, or a **Crab**,[32] and in her right hand a **dart**,[33] in her left, a looking glass clothed or covered with white or green and having on her

---

27 Now superseded by the King of the North, Egyn, who also bears serpentine heraldry.

28 Pseudo-Agrippa, p. 177.

29 Stratton-Kent, *The Testament of Cyprian the Mage*, p. 145.

30 Stephen Skinner & David Rankine, *The Keys to the Gateway of Magic: Summoning the Solomonic Archangels and Demon Princes* (Singapore: Golden Hoard, 2011).

31 Presented alongside a particularly fascinating conjuration of Hekate.

32 The astrological symbol of Cancer.

33 The dart is connected to the Greek Goddess Artemis and her role in the myth of Callisto, her companion, who was transformed into the constellation of Ursa Major by Zeus. Amaymon also bears this weapon in his description in *A Book of the Offices of Spirits*.

head **two serpents**[34] with **horns** twisted together, and to each arm a serpent twined about, and at each foot also"[35] [emphasis mine].

In conclusion, Asmodeus and his aliases, as well as the current King of the North, Egyn, both survive to the modern day bearing serpentine imagery within their descriptions as well as a consistent theme of being connected to the Gates of Cancer and Capricorn. The heraldry of Asmodeus is perhaps an echo of the astro-mythical event of the constellation Draco being overthrown as well as the importance of not only the North and the Pole Star being the location in which a great God of cosmogenic power is enthroned,[36] but also of the mysteries of the seven stars of both Ursa Major and Minor. This Spirit's heritage spans the gulf of human civilisation and connects us to our distant magical forebears and the cyclic, magical nature of Time. Finally, we can at least make some assumption that the nature of the Pole Star in the magic of Antiquity held a special role of astrological importance. All of creation orbits around the undying constellations of the Pole. Knowing its location and the mythology of creator Gods such as Aion and Abrasax, both of whom rule over Time alongside Cronus and his chaotic child, and Typhon as well as other cosmogenic Gods such as Mithras, and enthroning them upon this powerful mytho-location, the axis-mundi of the World, before making our calls upon the Spirits grants the sorcerer power over the entirety of creation.

> And the lord stood upon Tiamat's hinder parts,
> And with his merciless club he smashed her skull.
> He cut through the channels of her blood,
> And he made the North wind bear it away into secret places.[37]

---

34 Possibly a reference to the Agathos Daimon alongside their partner, Tyche, who are often depicted as serpents.

35 Skinner & Rankine, *The Keys to the Gateway of Magic*, p. 88.

36 Those familiar with the Stele of Jeu, a ritual designed to conjure the Headless One, will be familiar with the instruction to face the North. See PGM V. 96–172.

37 Leonard William King. *The Seven Tablets of Creation*. 1902. The Forth Tablet. Verses 129-132

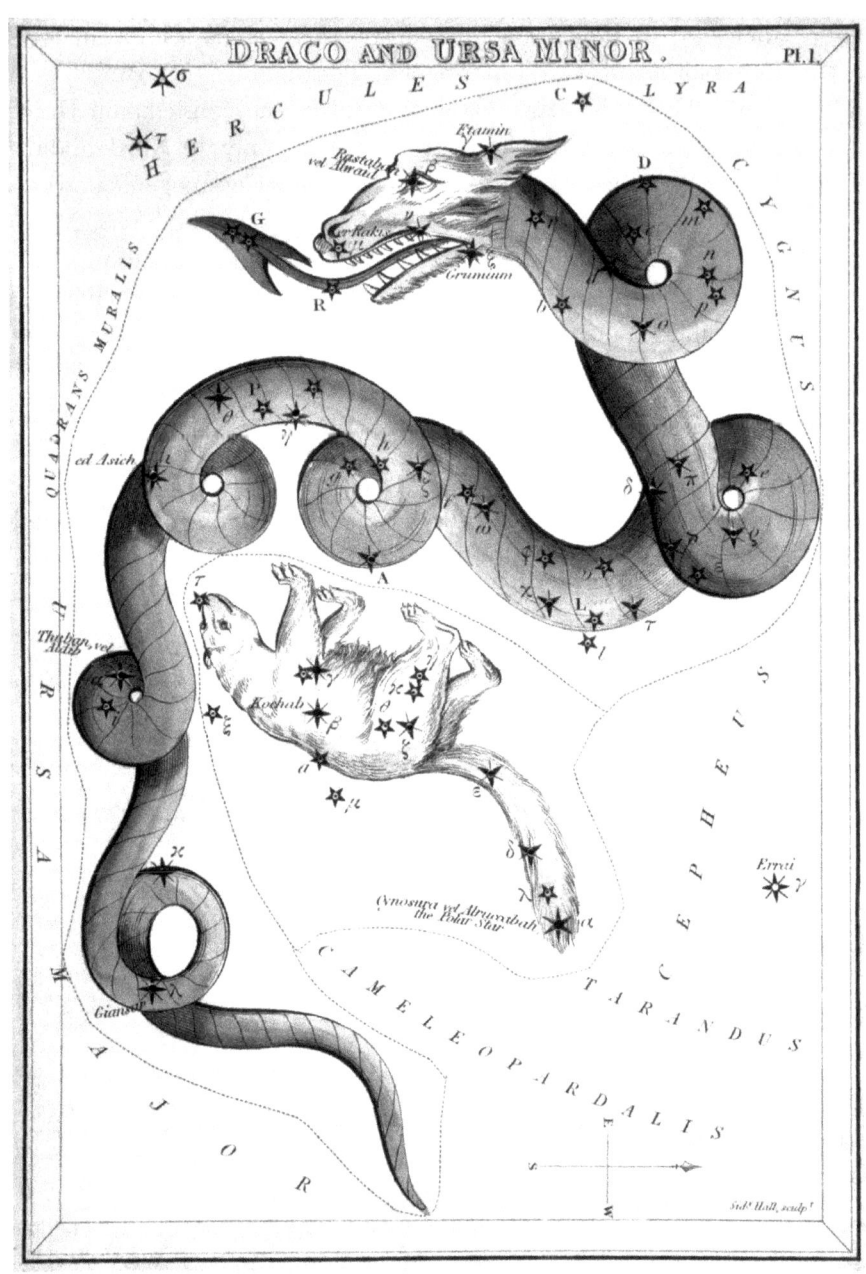

Fig.2: Urania's Mirror, Reverend Richard Rouse Bloxam, London, 1825.

✠
Four Kings

We see a large shake up occur when the four Kings as described by Cecco d'Ascoli's[38] infamous text on Astral Necromancy, *Commentary On the Sphere*, and later Antonio da Montolmo's, *On Occult and Manifest Things*[39] enter the hierarchies of the European grimoires and subvert or overthrow the older hierarchical positions and roles of *Hygromanteia*'s four directional Emperors: Lucifer, Belzebuth, Astaroth, and Asmodeus. It is from this point in the fourteenth century where we find our Four Kings explicitly connected to the astrological Cardinal Signs. Exactly how this revolution took place is unfortunately lost to history; however, from what evidence we do have we can see a blending of hierarchies occurring over time where previously Planetary Spirits found in the catalogues of the Hours became detached from their registers; new concepts and innovations were introduced, structures and roles of the hierarchies became more confused—if they ever actually held any real consistency—and while not exclusive, many of these confusions, corruptions, or omissions are found centred around the Spirit registers of the North.[40] We also find that in contrast to the many examples of corruption found in this quarter that many grimoires place a significant emphasis specifically on the conjuration of the North, with the Beralanensis conjuration found in the *Heptameron*[41] and later *Ars Goetia* being one such example which, while often assumed to be a generalised invocation, is instead specifically aimed towards the King of the North and the Tartarian Seat.

In the case of the *Grimorium Verum*, we find several points of interest when we compare it to the internal structure of *Hygromanteia*. Firstly, while many contemporary grimoires adopt Satan into their upper hierarchy, which has by this period of history become a Triumvirate or trinity, the *Verum* preserves Astaroth in her role as Chief. Asmodai, however, is completely omitted. As well as Asmodai's departure as ruler of the North,

---

38 1257-September 26, 1327, executed by the Inquisition.

39 A critical edition of which can be found in translation by Nicolas Weill-Parot in *Invoking Angels*, ed. by Claire Fanger, (University Park: Pennsylvania State University Press, 2012) pp 238-287.

40 According to Weill-Parot, the *Bibliotheca Philosophica Hermetica* explains that Oriens was witnessed in the Byzantine tradition of the Hygromantia Salomonis. (Weill-Parot, p. 287).

41 Pseudo-Agrippa, p. 71.

we see the Infernal Trinity maintain something of this Cardinality within the *Grimorium Verum* in their rulership over specific geographic regions of the world, namely Europe and Asia under Lucifer, Africa under Belzebuth, and the Americas under Astaroth. Outside the *Verum* we see Oriens, Amaymon, Paymon, and Egyn in their roles as Cardinal Zodiacal Kings come to the fore underneath this newly formed Infernal Trinity in later Elizabethan grimoires such as *The Book of Oberon*. The Kings come to replace their predecessors' prior roles as leaders of the Cardinal directions, while still having just enough ambiguity and unique personality to remain operational on an independent tier within the overall hierarchy. On top of this there are enough puzzles concerning the Northern catalogues, their differences from source to source, overtones of necromantic practices, alongside stellar lore and transmission issues which arise from this evolution, to fill an entire book. What we can say for certain is that this period of history saw a great revolution in Hell which transformed the magical topology found within the Grimoire Traditions of Europe.

Hygromanteia is an example of a text which has had a monumental influence upon the European magical tradition; having Greek roots in the *Testament of Solomon*, the final form of a much longer oral tradition which was codified between the first and fourth centuries of the Common Era, as well as being the carrier for an overwhelming amount of influence from the techniques and practices found within the Greek Magical Papyri, *Hygromanteia* went on to define the genre that became known as the Keys of Solomon. Its influences are glaring when studying texts such as *The Keys of Rabbi Solomon* (Wellcome MS 4670, Chapter XII)[42] and the *Heptameron* of Peter de Abano. What is more, while *Hygromanteia* is primarily a product of Byzantine culture, it is far from being purely so, with Christian overtones, Greek heritage, Jewish[43] influences, transmissions from Islamic[44] culture via *Picatrix*[45] and even tentative Vedic influences in parallels of technique based on the Lunar Mansions, it is truly a multicultural juggernaut of power

---

42 Published by Skinner & Rankine as *The Veritable Key of Solomon*.

43 Skinner & Rankine, *The Veritable Key of Solomon*, p. 58.

44 For example, by the association of Raphael with Thursday as well as the use of certain ingredients in fumigations found within the *Picatrix*.

45 Translated by Jewish scholar Yehuda ben Moshe into Latin and Castilian in the thirteenth century CE under the instruction of Alfonso X, in an effort to preserve Arabic and Hebrew astronomical and astrological knowledge. Ultimately this collective body of translated work positioned Castilian as a language of learning which forged the foundations of the modern Spanish language.

that went on to influence Dee and Kelly's Enochian system of magic, the *Grimorium Verum*, the *Ars Goetia*, and transform into something which has defined the modern magical landscape in ways we are only now coming to understand.

✠

The Aerial Spirits

And you hath he quickened, who were dead in trespasses and sins; Wherein in time past ye walked according to the course of this world, according to the prince of the power of the air, the spirit that now worketh in the children of disobedience:
Among whom also we all had our conversation in times past in the lusts of our flesh, fulfilling the desires of the flesh and of the mind; and were by nature the children of wrath, even as others.[46]

This text will examine five surviving manuscripts of the *Hygromanteia* which possess a highly detailed and systematic sequence of Names which have been lost from contemporary grimoire practice so that the modern sorcerer may further refine their practice. These Names are specifically those of the Hours of the Days of the week, totalling one hundred and sixty-eight. These Spirits, divided into the two categories of Angel and Demon, are in essence possessed of the admixtures of the *virtue*s which are in sympathy with the Seven Celestial Wanderers via the attribution of the Greek Gods they were paired with in the manuscripts of the *Hygromanteia*.[47] This is not to say these Spirits were thought of by the authors of these manuscripts to be *of* the Greek Gods specifically, as according to Marathakis, "Torijano argues that the prayers are adapted from a pagan source, since the planets are considered as actual divinities with certain attributes. However, if one looks carefully at these attributions, it is evident that they are purely astrological and have nothing to do with the pagan gods[…] The planets are not the recipients of the prayers, but natural forces conjured by the power of the One God, whether Christian,

---

46 Ephesians 2:1-3 (KJV).
47 See Skinner and Rankine, *The Veritable Key of Solomon*, p. 417: "The Planets themselves are not listed, instead they have been extrapolated from the Names of the Greek Gods."

Jewish or Neoplatonic."[48] This may indeed be the case for the authors of the *Hygromanteia*, but it should not prevent those of us interested in more pagan expressions of magic from engaging with this material. Nor does it require a belief in the One God or a Neoplatonic worldview. On the contrary, there is nothing preventing us from approaching these Spirits and their prayers in the same way a modern cunning man or woman may approach the magic of the Psalms, from the position of an Orphic, or even a modern Luciferian perspective. These Hours and their Spirits can just as easily be found to be consistent with modalities of practice based on the Greek Magical Papyri, with which a great many similarities exist.[49] These Names of the Hours are themselves a direct evolution of these very same techniques.

From a Pagan perspective, we find ourselves in agreement with Marathakis: the Spirits of the Hours presented here are not the Planets themselves, indeed, they shouldn't even be considered specifically Celestial, meaning they reside *above* the Moon. The Spirits which we are dealing with are Sub-Lunar, meaning they are active within the sphere of the Elements, the region we too inhabit. These Spirits are alternatively described as *Aerial*, meaning that they inhabit the region of space that exists between the Moon and the Earth. To quote Joseph H. Peterson, the Aerial Spirits, "Consist of a king and his assistants. The corresponding texts in CLM 849 use the term 'Kings of the spirits ruling and serving the seven days of the week.'"[50] Being *Aerial* doesn't mean the Spirits are purely of the Element of Air as described by the four classical Elements of Empedocles. Instead, these Spirits are the conscious, self-organising admixtures of Elemental properties which are found about the Earth, an umbrella region including the *Aerial*, *Terrestrial*, *Subterranean* and *Infernal*. Quoting from Chapter CXVII of *Liber Iuratus Honorii*, the earliest mentions of which date to the thirteenth century,

> The air is a corruptible element, fluid, and subtle, capable of receiving qualities from others, and is plainly invisible, but it is seen to be composed of parts of itself. In which are spirits, which the holy mother church calls damned, but they themselves assert

---

48 Marathakis, p. 50.

49 For example, see PGM IV. 1596-1715 & PGM VII. 862-918, the 'Consecration for all Purposes' and 'Lunar Spell of Claudianos and [ritual] of heaven and the north star over lunar offerings', respectively.

50 Peterson, *Elucidation of Necromancy*, p. 17.

the opposite to be true, and therefore we prefer to call them neither good nor evil. And those spirits that are governed by air act according to the nature of air itself, and therefore we can understand their nature. The air therefore, insofar as an element, is governed by the influences of the planets.[51]

Indeed, Greenfield describes at length the nature of these Spirits from the perspective of Byzantine religious thought,

> Another related concept that had appeared in much earlier traditions, was that of the demons inhibiting the air about the earth. It was supported by two passages from Ephesians in the New Testament, where the prince of the power of the air [...] is mentioned (2:2), apparently with reference to the Devil, and where the spiritual hosts of wickedness in the heavenly places [...] were included in the list of diabolical powers at 6:12.[52] This belief survived in the later tradition, which referred to the prince or princes of the air, and made the air the place of the Devil's rule on occasions; demons were to be found everywhere in it, flying and dwelling there, and occasionally appearing out of it to frighten men.[53]

The Greek Gods and the wandering stars to which these Spirits respond are but a reflection of the events occurring above, upon, and within the sphere of the Earth, and by their sympathetic *virtue*, they possess something of the nature of the Wanderer to which they have been ascribed. In this way, it can be seen that a Martial Spirit which we are engaging with is not *from* Mars or even *of* it, but instead possesses virtues and sympathies which exist in concordance with the nature or essence of this Planet within the *Aerial* Sphere. When Mars finds itself at home within Aries or Scorpio, or is exalted in Capricorn, it is as if a key has turned within a cosmic mechanism, meaning magical work done while Mars is within these regions of the sky

---

[51] Joseph H. Peterson, ed. and trans, *The Sworn Book of Honorius: Liber Iuratus Honorii* (Lake Worth: Ibis, 2016) p. 227.

[52] Ephesians (KJV) 6.12. "For we wrestle not against flesh and blood, but against principalities, against powers, against the rulers of the darkness of this world, against spiritual wickedness in high places."

[53] Richard P. H. Greenfield, *Traditions of Belief in Late Byzantine Demonology*, (Amsterdam: Hakkert, 1988), pp. 15-16.

possesses a nature which is in a deeper resonance with the aspects and qualities of this Planet. Such astrological timing, while highly beneficial and useful, is not strictly necessary. What matters is the Hour in which we do our work, as opposed to the aspects the Planets may be making with one another in the sky. Of course, a balance should be struck, but we can't always wait for the Planets to be in the most perfect place.

The Hours are permutations of each Wanderer focused as a lens by each Day, producing a model of the World as well as a map of *Time* through which the sorcerer may engage with the Aerial Spirits to effectuate change. When two Planets share friendship and are in union, for instance, Venus and the Sun on Friday, we find the Spirits which rule in this period of Time are capable of producing Love, which is part of the nature of the combination of these two Planetary forces. When Planets are in enmity, such as the Sun and Mars or the Sun and Saturn, we find their office to be the ominous, 'Do Nothing'. If we wish, we may develop this further by involving electional astrology. In fact, I would recommend it, especially when working with the Moon, who moves swiftly across the sky and transforms via Her phases. She acts as a Gatekeeper to the rest of the solar system, much as Saturn acts as Guardian and Gatekeeper to the Fixed Stars.

Fig.3: Saturnus.

✠
Thwarting Angels

Historically there is great precedence and many instances where an Angelic force is first conjured to restrain or 'thwart' a lower Demonic force, much as Raphael is described as doing to Asmodeus in the Testament of Solomon:

> And I adjured him by the name of the Lord Sabaôth, saying: "Fear God, Asmodeus, and tell me by what angel thou art frustrated." But he said: "By Raphael, the archangel that stands before the throne of God."[54]

Prior to Late Antiquity the divisions of Angel and Demon into distinct classes of Spirit with the modern connotations those words possess simply aren't found and are a decidedly Christian innovation. What we do find are *Angeloi* acting as Messengers[55] between the Divine and Mankind, as well as *Daimones* which often behave in a more personal manner. These Daimones are often responsible for either beneficial or malefic action, but are often indifferent or apathetic toward humanity. There is a great amount of ambiguity throughout history as the meanings of the words change. We find in Homer and many early Greek authors that even the Olympian Gods were referred to as *Daimones*.

> But when the loud-thunderer, the one who sees far and wide, heard this, he sent to Erebos [Hādēs] the one with the golden wand, the Argos-killer [Hermes], so that he may persuade Hādēs, with gentle words, that he allow holy Persephone to leave the misty realms of darkness and be brought up to the light in order to join the *daimones* [the gods in Olympus], so that her mother may see her with her own eyes and then let go of her anger.[56]

---

54 Conybeare, p. 21.

55 Ἄγγελος, meaning, 'messenger'. Compare to the Greek δαίμων, 'one who divides', 'dispenser', or 'tutelary deity'.

56 Anonymous, *Homeric Hymn to Demeter*, trans. by Gregory Nagy, Harvard Center for Hellenic Studies, 2018 <https://chs.harvard.edu/primary-source/homeric-hymn-to-demeter-sb/> [accessed 28 February 2024] (lines 334-339).

Even as late as the medieval grimoires "the terms are often used interchangeably."[57] We can say then that clinging to the strictly Christian modality doesn't necessarily serve any purpose and dispense with the unnecessary dichotomy which it has imposed upon us by the cultural zeitgeist of the era in which the texts were written. To quote from Book I of Stratton-Kent's *Geosophia*, specifically regarding the Demons found within the grimoire tradition, "A simple and effective strategy thereafter is to discard the old categories, and—largely ignoring the other types— approach the supposed demons in another way, seeing them as 'spirits', neither evil nor good as a genre, but each individually having their own particular nature."[58] We should add a further quote from Jake, "The grimoires are monuments of what may be called magic's 'interim period.' They are disfigured by a dualism which was not originally native to goetic tradition, but entered via a backdoor of changes in religion."[59]

Punitive methodologies are a mainstay of the sorcerous techniques of classical antiquity, many of which can be found in the threat narratives of the PGM and *Leyden Papyrus*, and while often expedient, they are not strictly compulsory. This isn't to say we should be careless in our approach to the Spirits; on the contrary, we should go to great pains to purify ourselves appropriately and to construct appropriate tools; especially the wands[60], knife, circle, and appropriate seals of protection such as a phylactery or lamen. Such things *are* a necessity. However, the techniques found in the European grimoires are not identical in nature entirely to those used in the Hellenic period and often seem to revel in torturing recalcitrant Spirits.[61] Thankfully there are enough examples of other, often more *infernal* methodologies which rely upon the correct employment of the hierarchy of Spirit, the feast and the signing of pacts. As such alternatives exist we may choose to engage with the Spirits in a far less aggressive manner, one

---

57 Peterson, *Elucidation of Necromancy*, p.17.

58 Jake Stratton-Kent, *Geosophia: The Argo of Magic*, vol. 1 (London: Scarlet Imprint, 2010) p.12.

59 Jake Stratton-Kent, *Pandæmonium: A Discordant Concordance of Diverse Spirit Catalogues* (West Yorkshire: Hadean Press, 2016) p. 239.

60 Of the Spirits Frimost and Klepoth if we are operating from within the framework of the *Grimorium Verum*.

61 A fantastic example of this methodology, as well as the diary entries which detail the reception of a unique grimoire by the infamous magicians Gilbert and Davis, can be read in Cummins and Legard's, *An Excellent Booke of the Arte of Magick*.

which recognises the potential danger which such magical work entails, while shunning the more vitriolic and spiteful modalities of many of the classical and mediaeval magicians. How we choose to engage with our magic and with our Spirits defines the type of sorcerer we wish to be and plays a vital role in the establishment and curation of our Spirit Court.

A further example which bears some significant similarity would be the Planetary Spirits described in Chapter XXII of Book II of Agrippa's *Three Books of Occult Philosophy*, which are presented alongside their Kameas, number squares which contain the virtues and properties of the Planets. We find the *Intelligence* of a Planet behaves as a mediating force, often equated with an Angel, while the Demon or *Spirit* is its active expression or Agent. Thus the 'Angels' and 'Demons' presented within this catalogue of Temporal Spirits from *Hygromanteia* can be recontextualised to fall into a similar modality. Both should be conjured during an operation, and tasked appropriately without the need for the modern moralistic baggage which has been accreted over them for the sake of sanity. This can be accomplished via the use of the Names of the Hierarchy through which they operate, by operating within their allotted Times, employing Divine Names of power woven into historiolae, and the manipulation of materia magica with sympathetic Elemental virtue alongside the use of sorcerous Voice and Action. In many ways the ability to perform these methods supersedes the use of simple violence and produces and establishes far better relationships between sorcerer and Spirit. We will find the Spirits respond well to mutually beneficial action while located and approached via the authority found within the ecology of their own hierarchical structure. As with any form of Spirit conjure, we begin by calling upon our principal Intermediary, through whom we then make our call to the highest Spirit at the top of a hierarchy such as a God, Chief, or King; then on to a Deputy, then to a Spirit, and then to whomever is tasked to the Sorcerer from the legions beneath them. We conjure the ruling Spirit to help us gain access to an audience with those that reside under its authority. By establishing a relationship with a Spirit or God who grants such authority to the sorcerer, we proceed to work together without the need for gratuitous threats or violence, while torture becomes completely redundant. A deeper relationship founded on respect becomes possible once this recontextualisation has been accomplished and we can be safe in the knowledge that the Spirits we employ do not fear, resent, and despise us.

Part III: Theory

✠

Determining the Hours

We should become fluent in our understanding of how the Hours themselves are generated, for they are never equal and change in length every day. Understanding how this process functions should be our first step.

In the catalogues that follow we will find the Spirits organised into seven sets of forty-eight, with two Spirits listed for each Hour of each Day and Night of the week. Each Hour begins at Dawn, meaning fifteen minutes before the disk of the Sun appears over the horizon.[62] The length of these Hours is uneven and changes as the Seasons progress, with longer Hours of Day in the Summer, and longer Hours of Night in the Winter. To know which Hour one is working in, first find the exact minute of Dawn and the exact minute of Twilight, the latter being fifteen minutes after the disk of the Sun has descended below the horizon. Determine how many minutes exist in that period of time and divide those minutes into twelve. Do the same for the Hours between Twilight and Dawn the next morning, and then double check that you have a total of exactly 1440 minutes. This will produce the unique spans of each Hour for the Day you are intending to work. Then, using the Chaldean Order of the Planets, being the apparent speed of motion through the sky from our vantage point upon the Earth from slowest to fastest, assign the Planet of the Day to the first Hour.[63] The first Hour of Saturday belongs to the God Kronos and the Planet Saturn, followed by Zeus and Jupiter in the second Hour, Ares and Mars in the third, followed by Helios and Sun in the fourth Hour, Aphrodite and

---

62 See Jake Stratton-Kent, *The True Grimoire*, 2nd ed. (London: Scarlet Imprint, 2023), p. 106: "In the day and hour of Mars, the Moon being at the crescent, and at the first hour of the day – which is a quarter of an hour before sunrise…"

63 Using the Chaldean (Babylonian) order in which the Planets are ordered we find the sequence begins with Saturn, the slowest and most distant of the Wanderers, and ends with the fastest and closest, the Moon. Saturn is domiciled within Capricorn, and the Moon in Cancer. Together these form a binary pole of their own which connect both Solstices, when the Sun is at its absolute height during the Summer in Cancer, and its nadir when night dominates in Capricorn. Collectively, these two points are connected to the horizon and the rising stars with the pole star being the axis upon which they are animated.

Venus in the fifth, Hermes and Mercury in the Sixth, and Selene and the Moon in the seventh. The pattern then repeats up to the twelfth Hour, we then continue the sequence onward for the twelve Hours of Night until all spaces have been assigned. The first Hour of each Day is always the Planet associated with it.

Once this process has been completed, the sorcerer may consult an ephemeris[64] to determine the astrologically significant events of the day. Events to look out for are hard aspects being made to the Planet you are considering working with, especially squares or oppositions with either Malefic, Mars or Saturn, or with mutable Mercury. This done the sorcerer may continue to design their ritual based around this timing, finding the most suitable time for their ritual, remembering that the first Hour of the Day while facing East is considered the quintessential best time for the creation of a talisman or activation of magic which can accomplish anything which holds sympathy with the virtues of the Planet concerned. Finally, it is notable to consider that while the first Hour of the Moon at Dawn on a Monday is the perfect time to deploy Lunar magic, the entire Day is Lunar in nature and each subsequent Hour is only a permutation of this Lunar quality, and so on this Day any Lunar quality can be worked with within this modality. The same goes for each Planet, with Tuesday being the Day of Mars, Wednesday being the Day of Mercury, etc.

Astrology is exceptionally useful when working with this form of magic and so other considerations should be taken into account: the Moon, specifically her waxing and waning phases, as well as taking note of which Planet is positioned on the Ascendant or Midheaven, making sure neither malefic inhabits those regions. Aspecting Planets can be utilised or avoided; it is also very useful to recognise when a particular Planet is in retrograde. Although retrograding Planets should not stop you from your work, you may have delayed results. Other issues which may occur include frustrations, setbacks, and miscommunications. Such astrological events do play a role in the outcome of the magic being worked and so a study of the night sky before any operation should be performed so as to be as informed as possible about what the potential fall out of any operation may be. The worst that can happen is a delayed result or simply nothing at all, but there are specific regions of Time, such as Via Combusta, known as 'the Burning Way', when the Moon is between fifteen degrees of Libra to fifteen degrees of Scorpio, which are very dangerous and can just as

---

64 A great resource for this is *Raphael's Astronomical Ephemeris*, published annually by W. Foulsham & Co. Ltd.

easily bring ruin upon the sorcerer as they can upon their enemies, if not handled well.

The Hours and their Spirits presented here have predominantly been used throughout history in the creation of talismans and image magic. It would be prudent to assume that this remains the case; however, just as it is necessary to conjure such Spirits to facilitate the creation of magical objects, their involvement in ritual could easily be adapted by the sorcerer to involve any form of magic we can conceptualise in the modern day. For example, if one is planning to open a business one could wait for the tenth Hour of Monday, being the Hour of Zeus-Jupiter on the Day of Selene, before this is done, or by going further and making a petition to the Spirit *Menaktinos* via *Sinael* during the Hour in which your new business opens. You will want to use a suitable blend of aromas and create an environment suitable for the reception of both Zeus and Selene, sing their Orphic Hymns, play specific types of music which evoke something of their combined virtue, welcome them humbly and with grace, and petition them through the Spirits of the Hour which you have conjured. Alternatively, the Spirits of the Hours could be conjured in a divinatory setting and questions asked so the sorcerer may gain insight into how and when a successful business could be created. Offerings to these Spirits could be made during their Hour four times during a lunar month in an effort to entice these Spirits to work with you, dream work could be initiated via mantra before sleep, or they could even be conjured during their Hour as one would with any other Spirit to learn details of their Seal, True Name and the Names of Spirits which make up their accompanying legions. Any form of practical Spellwork may be entertained when working with these Aerial Spirits, remembering that a Spirit's office is far broader than described in such catalogues and that whatever a Spirit can give, they can also take away.

✠

Friendship and Enmity

Each Planet possesses a unique *virtue* which describes its personality. These personalities are *Elemental* in nature, a philosophical as well as early phenomenological description of reality originating from the cosmogonic theory of the fourth-century BCE pre-Socratic philosopher Empedocles. This model of reality also presupposes the existence of *Love* and *Strife*, two forces which initiate or motivate the perpetual admixture of the Elements within the natural world. Agrippa describes, in Book I, Chapter XVII of his *Three Books of Occult Philosophy*, "Thus, in the elements, fire is against water and air is against earth. But [fire and air, and water and earth] agree with one another."[65] The Elements exist in permutation and can be divided into the admixtures of hot, dry, wet, and cold, which can be further attributed to the four *humours* or temperaments, those being *choleric*, *phlegmatic*, *sanguine*, and *melancholic*. These in turn were each attributed to specific forms of bodily fluids in the medicine of Hippocrates: the yellow bile, phlegm, blood, and black bile, which correspond to hot and dry, cold and wet, hot and wet, and cold and dry, respectively.

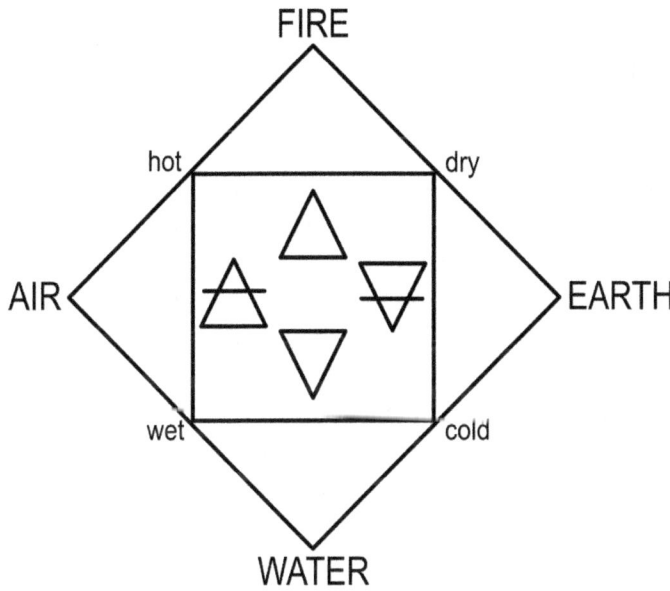

Fig.4: Elements.

Each Planet, then, is an expression of a permutation of the Elements, which in combination produce their *virtue*, that being their innate substance or essence. These virtues form the building blocks of every substance, visible or invisible, that can be found in the natural world and form the basis of astrology and astrological magic from antiquity through the Renaissance, to the modern day. Each Planet possesses certain positive and

---

65 Heinrich Cornelius Agrippa, *Three Books of Occult Philosophy*, Vol. I, ed. and trans. by Eric Purdue (Rochester, VT: Inner Traditions, 2020) p. 65.

negative traits, the same as any human personality, and are locked into perpetual motion. They are actors upon the stage of the night sky, each moving through the twelve Signs of the Zodiac and the Houses which define the scenes through which their play is expressed. As each Planet moves into a new Zodiacal Sign it may find itself within its domicile, exaltation, fall, or detriment. These terms describe the waxing and waning of each Planet's virtue, which is coloured by the elemental composition of the Zodiacal Sign in which they currently inhabit. Mars finds itself at home or domicile within both Aries and Scorpio; these are the seats of his power, and so during these times his virtues are heightened and strong, with Mars being seen as beneficial while in Aries but malignant while in Scorpio. In contrast, while Mars inhabits the sign of the Bull, Taurus, he finds himself in detriment or exile, his powers at their nadir. Collectively these combinations are known as the Planetary Dignities.

Finally, the *aspects* the Planets make as they move through the scenes of the cosmic play, those being the angles or degrees of relationships present within an astrological chart, such as conjunctions, oppositions, squares, trines, and sextiles, are the expressions of the interactions being made between the actors, with hard angles such as oppositions at 180° or square at 90° being seen as antagonistic, while soft angles such as trines at 120° or sextiles at 60° being harmonious. Each Planet is part of an intricate sequence of relationships similar to a dramatic play, with games of power, subterfuge, and romance being expressed via their interactions. From studying these evolving relationships and dynamics we can predict moments of time in which we may plant our magical actions in the most fertile soil.

Each Planet which includes the Sun and the Moon are friends with some, indifferent to a few, and enemies of others. There are three categories of Planet, the *Luminaries* Sun and Moon, the *Benefic* Venus and Jupiter, the *Mutable* Mercury, and the *Malefic* Mars and Saturn. It would be wonderful if I could now present a single, entirely agreed upon model of these interweaving relationships upon which all astrologers from the Middle Ages to the present day agree upon; however, this is unfortunately far from the case. Below you will find four examples, taken from different cultures presented in chronological order in which they were written and leave the exact interpretation of this information to the reader.

Al-Biruni - 11th Century[66]

PLANET	FRIENDSHIP	ENMITY	INDIFFERENCE
☉	♃ ♂ ☽	♄ ♀	☿
☽	☉ ☿	n/a	♄ ♃ ♂ ♀
☿	☉ ♀	☽	♄ ♃ ♂
♀	♄ ☿	☉ ☽	♃ ♂
♂	♃ ☉ ☽	♄ ♀	☿
♃	♂ ☉ ☽	♀ ☿	♄
♄	♀ ☿	♂ ☉ ☽	♃

MS Gennadianus 45 - 16th Century[67]

	FRIENDS			ENEMIES	
☉		♂	☉		♄
♄		♃	♄		☽
☽		♀	☽		♂
♂		☿	♂		♃
This way you can learn everything		♃			☿
		♀			

Agrippa - 1533 CE[68]

PLANET	FRIEND	ENEMY
☽	♀ ♃ ♄	☿ ♂ (☽)
♂	♀	☉ ☿ ☽ ♃ ♄
☿	♀ ♃ ♄	☉ ☽ ♂
♃	☉ ☿ ♀ ☽ ♄	♂
♀	☉ ☿ ♀ ☽ ♃	♄
♄	☉ ☿ ☽ ♃	♂ ♀
☉	♃ ♀	♂ ☿ ☽

---

66 Chart compiled from Al-Biruni, *The Book of Instructions in the Elements of the Art of Astrology*, trans. by R. Ramsay Wright (London: Luzac, 1934; repr. Bel Air, MD: Astrology Classics, 2006).

67 Compiled from Marathakis, p. 305.

68 Compiled from Agrippa, p. 65.

	♄	♃	♂	☉	♀	☿
William Lilly - 1647 CE[69]						
☽	Enemies	Friends	Enemies	Friends	F / E[70]	Friends
☿	Friends	Friends	Friends	Enemies	Friends x	
♀	Enemies	Friends	Friends	Friends		
☉	Enemies	Friends	Friends			
♂	Enemies	Enemies				
♃	Friends					

To quote from Marathakis, "The logic of these talismans (of the Hours) is usually combinative. For instance, Venus traditionally pertains to operations regarding love, while Saturn is often attributed to operations aiming to harm. Thus, a talisman made during the fourth hour of Friday, which has Venus as a ruler of the day, and Saturn as a ruler of the hour, will prevent love between two persons."[71]

We may then utilise the charts of Friendship and Enmity as found above to help us in judging and interpreting how we translate the specific permutations of Planetary virtues found in the Lists of the Hours and proceed accordingly as best we see fit. Doing so will reveal something of the intuitive patterns of the offices which emerge from the lists as we explore them. Grasping the underlying principles of the Hours of the Days of the week, knowing their Names and exactly when to engage with them during ritual for best effect remains largely absent from modern reconstructions of the grimoire tradition. Marathakis goes on to say, "It could be also contended that this section in the *Magical Treatise* is the source of every grimoire that uses the planetary hours."[72]

---

69 Compiled from William Lilly, *Christian Astrology*, Books 1 & 2, ed. by David R. Roell (London: Macock, 1647; repr. Bel Air, MD: Astrology Classics, 2005). This was the first compendium of astrological lore and technique to be published in English as opposed to Latin. Lilly went on to become one of the most influential authors on the subject of astrology in the early modern period. His contributions to the field continue to be felt to the present day.

70 It should be noted that the Moon in its waxing phase is adverse to Venus.

71 Marathakis, p. 37.

72 Marathakis, p. 40.

The Dignitaries and Virtues of the Planets

Each Planet has four Dignitaries within the Zodiac, which are expressions of its strength and relationships as it traverses the sky throughout the year. The best way to describe this relation is to use the example of the Sun, whose power is renewed when entering Aries on the Vernal Equinox. From this point onwards the Sun is rejuvenated and begins to once more rise in power, warming the world and ending the Winter. Thus, the Sun is said to be Exalted in Aries and in Fall on entering Libra, the opposite point of the Zodiac. The Sun rules the Fixed Sign Leo, where it is at the height of its power at the peak of Summer; this is known as the Sun's Domicile or Home. The opposite position of the chart from Leo is Aquarius, where the Sun is considered in Detriment, the nadir of its power and influence and the coldest region of the seasons. Precession has shifted the path of the Sun over the centuries, meaning the exact dates of the Equinoxes and Solstices have moved in relation to the stars and so represent the Zodiacal year, not the calendar year. Each of the Planet's dignitaries are described in the charts below.

Planetary Dignities				
Sign	Domicile	Exaltation	Fall	Detriment
♈	♂	☉ 19°♈	♄	♀
♉	♀	♀ 3°♉		♂
♊	☿			♃
♋	☽	♃ 15°♋	♂	♄
♌	☉			♄
♍	☿	☿ 15°♍	♀	♃
♎	♀	♄ 21°♎	☉	♂
♏	♂		☽	♀
♐	♃			☿
♑	♄	♂ 28°♑	♃	☽
♒	♄			☉
♓	♃	♀ 27°♓	☿	☿

The Sun rules over all favour and authority, judgements, and retributions. His light shines upon every dark and hidden place, revealing secrets and treasures. The Sun is the primary Luminary, but is also a Mutable Planet, meaning its behaviour is changeable depending on which other Planets He makes aspect with. He is shining, bright, and powerful in all things.

The Moon rules over all secrets and hidden things, sorcery, and mystery. She subdues enemies and is good for trading and the exchange of money. She is the lesser Luminary, and is also Mutable as the Sun. She rules over illusion and dreams. Together with the Sun, she holds sway over inspiration.

Mars is a warrior. He rules over war, violence, and slaughter. When approached well he teaches courage, honour, pride, strength of body and mind, regimen, and protection. He is the lesser Malefic and can cause great harm, but also lends his force in overcoming obstacles and adversary.

Mercury is the swift traveller and psychopomp. His powers reach from the Celestial to the Underworld. He rules over all wisdom and knowledge, education, skill, and communication, but is also a silver-tongued God and prone to deception. Mercury is purely Mutable and so takes on the virtue of the Planets he makes aspect with.

Jupiter is the fruitful God. He is the lord of prosperity, vigour, generation, guidance, and health. He glorifies mankind. Jupiter is the greater Benefic and his bounty and wealth comes to all those who call upon or make aspect with Him.

Venus is the Goddess of love, passion, kindness, and nurturing affection. She brings grace, harmony, and benevolence to those who would call Her. She is the lesser Benefic and distributes her joy to those that make aspect with Her.

Saturn is the dour wanderer, the slow guardian who roams the cold vastness at the very boundary of the spheres. While he rules over death and decomposition, he also rules over structure and form. He reigns within the fallow earth, rich in potential. He is the wisest and most venerable of the Planets, the Greater Malefic, He brings binding, destruction, restriction, and misery to those He makes aspect with.

✠
DIS-ASTAR

Taking some time to explore the emergent patterns which express themselves throughout the reconstructed catalogue, we discover several interesting phenomena. A comparison will reveal that many of the *Dangerous Hours* which implore us to, *do nothing* or, *be careful*, have solid hemerological reasonings based on the *friendship* and *enmity* of the Planetary virtues involved. Despite some entries warning us not to work in these Hours we find that there are just enough cases in which suggestions are made that there is justification in tentative experimentation in various forms of magic during these times. An example of such an unfortunate Hour is the second Hour of Monday, which MS Harleianus 5596 suggests is good *For sickness*, whereas both the texts of Monacensis Gr.70 and Gennadianus 45 state that it is simply a *Bad hour*, or a *Bad and useless hour*, respectively. From such a brief description we can't be sure if the sickness suggested is one meaning, *to cure one of sickness* or not; however, given the second Hour of the Day of the Moon is under the aegis of Saturn, the Greater Malefic, we can assume that all forms of sickness are accessible through this Hour and that it may mean that sickness could be cast as a curse against one's enemies or cured in equal measure. There is also the possibility that the Hour is itself considered *contagious* if worked with and that sickness may befall the sorcerer if certain steps aren't taken to prevent such dangers. Having a suitable level of protection while working under these malefic Hours becomes an absolute necessity. We also see the lesser malefic Mars, having its fair share of *useless hours*, although just as with Saturn, we see something of its Martial nature making its way into some entries, examples being the fourteenth Hour of Sunday which is suitable for *preventing an address*, or the nineteenth Hour of Wednesday which is good for *making retribution*. Extending these ideas out further, we can assume that the instances in which we are instructed to *do nothing*, given they have attendant Spirits, definitely have power over particularly malefic offices which, being brave enough, we may attempt.

By the same token, *be careful* appears to be a separate and perhaps even inviting category, quite separate from instances of *do nothing*. We aren't being forbidden from an action, only warned, much in the same way as the instances of entries where we are told the Hour is *bad* or *dangerous*. *Do no work* is less of a warning and more a suggestion not to perform physical labour or work on one's projects or livelihood. We find this office in connection with

Saturn and thus the Sabbath. The *dangerous hour* is given, not surprisingly, on the Day of Mars in the Hour of Saturn and an alternative reading of this Hour's office suggests *causes conflict* which, given our understanding of Planetary friendship and enmity, makes a lot of sense. We aren't being told not to perform any magic in this Hour, only that whatever we do should be done with great care and attention to detail, lest we bring ruin upon ourselves.

A *useless hour* is also to be understood differently from *do nothing*, as they appear in instances where the Planetary dignities at play cancel each other out. An example being the second Hour of Night on a Thursday, the Hour of Saturn, which limits, inhibits or creates boundaries around the innately expansive forces of Jupiter. This may be *useless* for the creation of an active talisman, but it may be an opportunity for the sorcerer to explore the nature of the relationship between these two Planets and learn something from their interactions. *Useless* is also found on the Night of Mars in the Hour of the Sun, this being because the vitalising virtue of the Sun is absent, meaning the Martial essence of the Hour is either literally useless in that it is impotent, much as the interplay of Jupiterian and Saturnian forces described above, or perhaps because the virtues of this Hour are horrifically malefic, to the point where any attempt to utilise such an Hour would only ever produce something awful, destructive, and hateful, with absolutely no benefit to anyone, save potentially some truly awful curse.

There is a single instance of an Hour's office being, *Very Malign*, and we find this on the Night of Saturn in the Hour of Mars, a permutation of both lesser and greater Malefics. What stands out is that the first Hour of Mars on this same day rules over the "setting up of enchantments". Thus we can't say that universally such permutations are utterly out of bounds to the sorcerer. There must be some potential operant facility the Spirits of these Hours are capable of, even if the authors of the manuscripts were not willing to describe them.

Finally it should be underscored here that whatever a Spirit can give it can just as easily take away, so when for instance we find the fourth Hour on a Friday is ruled by Saturn and whose office is described as *Obstacles of Love*, we find that this Hour can be worked with to either cause obstacles or remove them. The other permutations of Venus and Saturn on this day are, *do nothing*, *sending dreams of hatred*, and *restraining love*. We can see the disastrous virtues of these Hours and how they could be used to cause great harm or suffering, but there is always the option to instead aid ourselves, remove obstacles which prevent us from expressing our love to those we care for, to heal from trauma which prevents us from sleeping well, and to find healthy boundaries of love which help us grow and better come to understand and love ourselves.

Each Hour can be called on and worked with in any way deemed fit, from the creation of magical items, to divination, to the evocation of Spirits or other forms of practical spell work. Experimentation is vital just as much as an open mind and a willingness to work with the Spirits to uplift ourselves and others. All this said, there is a reason these Hours were listed in this way and the bold sorcerer should take great care and pay particular attention to the details of the Circle, the Knife, and the Lamen, as well as consulting an ephemeris to determine the best astrological times such dangerous experiments may take place.

✠

The 12 Signs of the Zodiac and their Virtues

The following is a composite of several documents, namely MS Neapolitanus II C. 33, which is missing entries for Capricorn through Pisces, the more complete MS Parisinus Gr. 2419, and the astrologically rich MS Atheniensis 1265. This has been done to create a more holistic representation of potential applications available during these periods of time. The best time for creating such talismans or conjuring the Spirits involved with them is while the Sun and Moon are well-aspected in the heavens and not afflicted by Mars or Saturn. Both Malefics should also not be found on the Ascendant or at Midheaven. The Moon should be waxing to produce talismans of increase and waning for decrease.

A sympathetic day and Hour may also be chosen. For instance, Tuesday can be a profitable time to work with Aries or Scorpio as Mars rules in both. Working within the Hour of Mars will add greatly to the talisman's potential, even more so if Mars is inhabiting the Sign, although one should be especially careful with either Malefic. These extra considerations may help greatly although they are not strictly necessary.

In many instances below we find a Planetary Hour being recommended for certain actions. Given our understanding of Planetary Friendship and Enmity as well as knowing the Names and offices of the Spirits which preside over those Hours, we are left with a highly intricate and powerful system of astrological magic. Aries begins the sequence as it is the beginning of the astrological year, marked by the vernal equinox.

Aries is useful for making a parchment talisman to carry in the presence of kings, lords, officials, and generals. It will bring you power and glory. It is beneficial for selling, for learning and teaching an art, for asking for a gift or favour from those in authority or friends, and for travelling by Sea if made during the Hour of the Sun or Mercury.

Taurus is useful for making a talisman of love and friendship in the hour of Venus, who rules this Sign. It is also good for asking a favour from a beloved woman, or for harming her.

Gemini is ruled by the Sun and Saturn. It is useful for the education of children if made during the hour of Saturn; for making agreements of marriage, and for beneficial judgements and speaking with a powerful person. It is also good for harvesting herbs during the hours of Mars or Mercury.

Cancer is useful for hunting and is ruled by the Moon. It is also good for making a parchment talisman against demons and to help the possessed if made during the Hour of Mercury. In the Hour of Jupiter it is useful for the breaking and destruction of sorceries.

Leo is useful for slaying one's enemies and for making parchment or another kind of talisman to restrain those that would speak ill of you. It is also good for making a parchment talisman to carry during war or for displaying one's skill with a sword[73] when made during the Hour of Mars.

---

73 This ability is listed under the purview of Cancer in A but of Leo in both N and P.

Virgo is ruled by Mercury and is useful for bringing the Spirits within a water pot or bottle, and for interrogating them about hidden treasure if made during the Hour of Saturn. It is also good for gathering the Spirits and for speaking with them in[74] the Circle.

Libra is ruled by the Sun and useful for intimidating someone and for causing dreams, and for sending dreams from a woman to a man or the opposite when made during the Hour of the Sun. Such a talisman is also useful for reconciling enemies, for calming an estranged couple, preserving the peace between lovers, and preventing the temptation of a third person if made in the Hour of Mercury (Venus or Jupiter).[75]

Scorpio is ruled by Mars and is useful for destroying one's enemies, for harming the productivity of a workshop, and for binding men when made in this Hour. For unbinding and for making a parchment talisman in order not to fear one's enemies, do the same in the Hour of the Moon.

Sagittarius is ruled by the Moon and useful for making sown fields fruitful and rich. If you hold silver, gold, or other coins during this sign, they will multiply. It is also useful for preventing someone from harming his enemies, in confessing to friends, and in order to fear no one while seeming great and fearsome.

Capricorn is ruled by Saturn and is useful for destroying one's enemies together with their whole families if made during the Hour of Mars. It is also good for making two beloved friends hate each other if made in the Hour of Saturn.

---

74 Interestingly, this is described as inside, not outside as is normally found within such descriptions.

75 There is a difference among all three texts.

Aquarius is also ruled by Saturn and is useful for making a parchment talisman in order not to fear the sea. If the talisman is made in the Hour of Mercury the seas will be calmed. Such a talisman can also be used for making a strong and powerful binding friendship and love in the hour of…[76]

Pisces is ruled by Jupiter and Mercury. It is useful for making a parchment talisman in order to win at dice or similar games of chance if made in the Hour of Mercury. Such a talisman can also render oneself invisible. Talismans made using this Sign will aid in practising skull divination, water divination and similar.

---

76 Presumably Venus.

Part IV: Lunar Hemerology

✠

Concerning the Dragon who resides in the Ninth Heaven

The following is taken directly from Marathakis' translation of MS Atheniensis 1265 and offers us a means whereby the astrologer may interpret the 'movement' of the constellation of Draco, or Caput Draconis, which consists of the four stars Eltanin, Rastaban, Kuma, and Grumium. These four movements determine if one of four disasters will occur *in the whole world*. The original date given in the manuscript is the 13th of March, which was the date of the vernal equinox in the 14th or 15th century when this was most likely written. Today however, due to precession, the current date of the spring equinox is the 20th of March and so the following has been updated. While the section in A which immediately precedes the description of the Ninth Heaven appears to be discussing the Lunar Nodes, those being the points in the sky where the orbit of the Moon intersects the plane of the ecliptic,[77] the original author attributes this instead to a higher sphere of the geocentric model which resides above the Fixed Stars and has a relationship with Saturn, possibly as the guardian of the celestial threshold but almost certainly as the Lord of Time. What's more, there is a fascinating connection with this methodology to the Pole Star, the constellation Draco, and the two Gates which flank it, namely Cancer and Capricorn, which together threads through our examination of Time, a through-line which connects the magical practice of the Greek Magical Papyri with the Late Byzantine grimoires.

> There is a ninth heaven that is called starless, because it does not have stars. But there is a sole star in it, in the likeness of a Snake. It surrounds this heaven completely. Four actions take place within this star. Sometimes it opens its mouth and yawns, sometimes it moves and clicks its tongue, sometimes it shakes its tail, and sometimes its middle parts. Behold, the actions bring four effects. When it yawns, it shows death. Because, when yawns, it shows that the earth will receive human bodies. When it clicks

---

77 Used to determine the points at which the two Luminaries form a conjunction, i.e., an eclipse, a highly malefic event.

its tongue, it foretells war, because its tongue is sword-like. When it shakes its tail, hunger will take place on the whole earth. And when it quivers its middle parts, it reveals great earthquakes.

This is the explanation: Behold four signs of the Zodiac that are in conformity with the snake: Cancer, Leo, Scorpio and Capricorn. Watch and observe the day of March when the Sun enters Aries. Find the position of the Moon on this day. If the Moon is in one of the aforementioned signs on the 20th of March, you may know that the snake gave one of his signs for this year. If the moon is in Cancer on the 20th of March, you may know that the snake yawns and it shows death. If the Moon is in Leo, the snake has clicked its tongue which means war in the whole world. If the Moon is in Scorpio on the 20th of March, you may know that the snake has quivered its middle parts foretelling great earthquakes in the world. Finally, if the Moon is in Capricorn on the 20th of March, you may know that great hunger will take place upon the whole earth. If you calculate this with accuracy, you can predict the future without failing.[78]

For those interested, the Moon will be at 5 degrees of Leo at 06:07 GMT on the 20th of March 2024 which does not bode well; however, it will be at 5 degrees of Sagittarius in 2025, 15 degrees of Aries in 2026, barely within Virgo at 0 degrees in 2027, unfortunately at 27 degrees of Capricorn in 2028, then finally 25 degrees of Taurus in 2029 and 7 degrees of Libra in 2030. Let's hope for the best.

☦

The Beneficial Days of the Moon

The following table is our first example of sorcerous Καταρχα, that being the magical application of specific favourable times or *Beginnings*, and what I would like to propose as a model of hemerology which the magicians of today may utilise and hopefully upon which develop in the future. These Days are unique to the Moon and have been taken from MS Atheniensis 1265. Although a glimpse of a more complete Lunarium which includes the Names of ruling Angels

---

78 Marathakis, pp. 255-56.

and Demons can be found in MS Atheniensis 115, sadly all but the first fourteen pairs have been lost.

The Days of the Moon, at least in modern astrological lore concerning the Mansions, are divided into 28 positions of the night sky, with three Mansions per Zodiacal Cardinal Sign and two each for the remaining Fixed and Mutable. The following Lunar Days and their descriptions may have some tenuous connection to this practice, but are perhaps best understood as being a separate system of hemerological *katarchai*, as they are simply the *Days of Lunation*, meaning a measure of the amount of light being cast upon the Moon's surface as opposed to being specifically connected with its location in relation to the fixed stars. The primary, albeit tenuous, thread which connects these Lunar Days with the Mansion is the influence of the game of chess, which, alongside the Mansions, has its possible origins on the Indian subcontinent some 1500 years ago.[79] Depending on the system of the Mansions we find twenty-eight or twenty-nine divisions, with the former becoming the most commonly utilised today due to its symmetry. The Lunar month and its calendars however are usually twenty-nine days in length, making for a series of twelve lunations per year within a cycle of 354 days, eight hours, forty-eight minutes, thirty-four seconds.

MS Atheniensis 1265 details favourable ritual actions that may be enacted while engaging with the Moon during these fortunate Days. These offices, for want of a better word, are detailed below. The methodology is also described for the other Planets and involves the conjurations of specific Spirits which rule over the Day. These will be detailed for each Planet in their own sections and constitute a simple and thorough system of practical astrological magic.

---

[79] There is, however, evidence that systems of Lunar Mansions have evolved independently in multiple cultures.

The Lunations of the Moon and their Offices	
Day	Office
The 1st Day of the Moon	Lucky for gambling and games of luck
The 2nd Day	For Gain and Winning Chess
The 3rd Day	For Making Talismans for War
The 4th Day	For Causing Love
The 5th Day	Causing Love of Kings and Lords
The 6th Day	For Beneficial Judgement
The 7th Day	For Divining with a Water Pot
The 8th Day	For Finding Treasures within the Earth
The 9th Day	For Family Happiness and Household Issues
The 10th Day	For Epilepsy
The 11th Day	For Making Children Obey their Father
The 12th Day	Making Fathers Love their Children
The 13th Day	For Increasing Property
The 14th Day	For Seeing and Subjugating Spirits
The 15th Day	For Speaking with Demons
The 16th Day	For Making a Man Love his Wife
The 17th Day	For Restraining a Boat from Sailing
The 18th Day	To Make a Woman Confess
The 19th Day	For Opening Locks
The 20th Day	For Destroying Enemies and Opponents
The 21st Day	For Binding the Evil Tongue
The 22nd Day	For Unbinding Sorceries
The 23rd Day	For Fishing
The 24th Day	To not Fear Punishment
The 25th Day	For Binding or Unbinding a Couple
The 26th Day	For Compelling Enemies and Masters
The 27th Day	For Love and Bindings of Love
The 28th Day	For Love
The 29th Day	For Destruction

Concerning the Lunar observations of a Persian philosopher named Zanatēs

The following has been paraphrased extensively from Marathakis's translation of MS Neapolitanus II C.33. These observations are separate from the Lunations of the Moon described above and are far more related to the system of Mansions, however only superficially so. These Καταρχή are also less specifically sorcerous and are far more related to practical advice and suggested physical actions to be taken while the Moon is in a certain region of the sky, while also offering some form of prognostication in predicting the temperaments of children born during these times, the outcome of marriages, and matters of theft, sickness, or the health of a woman if she attempts an abortion.

Many of the specific points of advice do not apply or sit well with us in the modern age and so in some cases the language used has been updated to reflect modern sensibilities. In other instances, advice such as, *Today is a good day to buy slaves* has been left as an example of the type of people likely using this form of hemerology and the time in which it was written. Despite the overt sexism throughout against women, and prejudice against Geminis, the content of Zanatēs' prognostications are, given the climate in which they were written, surprisingly positive in many regards, especially with the concern granted to the health of women seeking abortion. Unfortunately, this is spoiled by the focus of happiness in marriage being almost exclusively placed on the man. Reading between the lines we can attempt to re-conceptualise these specific prognostications to apply to our lives in the modern age. Taking our understanding of Planetary Dignities and Zodiacal Virtues, we may even attempt to produce our own set of Lunar Observations and supersede Zanatēs entirely.

The Moon in	Office
♈	Beneficial for foreign rulers, navigators and travellers. Travel, and you will return joyous. Those that marry will have untidy and unloving partners. Do not attempt abortion; recovery will be difficult. The Second Day[80] is good for buying. Those taken by a sickness will recover but suffer headaches. The fugitive will be found. This is a fruitful time: sow and work the earth. Make foundations. The stolen object will be found. A child born this day will become a perjurer. Educate children. Good for family affairs.
♉	Regarding travel, the emigrant will return. Good for buying, speaking in public, making friends, and rest. Marriage will be unhappy and plagued by infidelity. Abortion is dangerous. The sick will hardly recover. The fugitive and the stolen object will be found. Children born on this day will not be happy. The Moon is Exalted and rejoices.
♊	The emigrant remains in the foreign land for a long time. Good for travelling back to your country. Marriages will be happy. Abortion is dangerous. Do not buy, sell, or lend. People who sicken on the First Day will hardly recover, but those that sicken on the Second will recover quickly. It will take a long time, but the fugitive will be found; the stolen object will be found quickly. Men conceived or born will be ugly, of bad character, and will not bring any good to their parents. If a woman is born, she will be unlucky and separate from her husband and parents. Born on the Second Day, men will be slow to understand but rich and women will be pleasant and intelligent. Those imprisoned will remain so for a long time.
♋	In travel, you shall be successful. If you stay in foreign places for a long time you will return joyfully. Whoever marries shall be ashamed of their partner. Abortions will be safe. The fugitive will be found. The ill person will recover swiftly. Men born will become experienced artisans, learned, happy, and rich.

---

80 "The Second Day", presumably the second day in which the Moon inhabits this Sign, is another potential hint at the connection to the system of Lunar Mansions.

Part IV: Lunar Hemerology

♌	On the First Day do not travel far; there will be bad luck. The Second Day is not much better. Do not marry, for your partner will be proud, irritable, and insubordinate. Abortion is dangerous. The fugitive will not be found. Beneficial for sowing. Those imprisoned will remain longer than they should. Men born will be rich and powerful, but cruel. Women born will have a tendency for sex work.
♍	The emigrant will remain away for a long time but return safely. Do not marry a virgin; it is better to marry a widow. Abortion is dangerous. The fugitive will remain at large for the First Day, but will be found on the Second. Sow crops but do not plant trees. The prisoner will be free soon. The stolen object will be found. Men born on the First Day will be learned, cunning, and rich. Women will be sickly. Men born on the Second Day will be merchants prone to drink and be soft, lazy, slanderous, and amorous. Women will be slanderous, tending to adultery, and lascivious, amorous and immoral.
♎	Good deeds will be fruitless, but crimes shall be successful. Do not marry: there will be adultery. Sickness this day will be very serious. Abortion is dangerous. The fugitive will be caught, the stolen object will be found. The prisoner will be free soon. Sow, plant, and prune. Men born on the First Day will be prudent, yet fond of sex workers and travel. Women will be prudent and loving and have a stable mood. All children born on the Second Day will only live a few years.
♏	Travel will be profitable. If you marry on the First Day, the Second Day will see adultery. Those that become sick will be cured. The fugitive will be found. The prisoner will be free soon. Men born on the First Day will be sorrowful, and women will be heartless and liars. Men born on the Second Day will be witty and firm, while women will be prudent and happy.

♐	The emigrant will return quickly. If he returns, he will find happiness soon. Good for marriage: one's partners will be faithful and loving. Sickness will be cured swiftly. The fugitive will not be found. Do not sow. The stolen object will not be found. The prisoner will soon be free. Children born on the Second Day will live long lives; they will be happy, powerful, and energetic, but also irritable.
♑	Do not travel abroad, you will find discomfort and sorrow. Returning home will be easy and profitable, especially those who travel and trade by sea. If a person intends to marry, then the second matchmaking is best as the man will be calm and the woman affectionate. The sick will be cured soon. The stolen object will be found. Those that move house on the First Day will be rich and happy. Those born on this day will be happy and admirable. Those born on the Second Day will be useless and not live long.
♒	Do not travel on the First Day. The Second Day will be profitable and advantageous. It furthers someone to buy slaves. Marriage is good: there will be affection between partners. Abortion on the First Day is dangerous. Sow and plant. The fugitive will be found. Men born on the First Day will be lewd and lascivious. Children born on the Second Day will be happy.
♓	It is good to travel and sail for commerce. It is also good to start a war. Good for hunting. Marriage is good, as the partners will be faithful, loving, and obedient. The sick person will not be in danger. The fugitive will be in danger and will return. The stolen object will be found. Sow, plant, build, and count. Children born on this day will be obedient, healthy, and happy.

The Beneficial & Malign Days of the Month

The following chart of beneficial and malign days of the month is found in folio 23 of MS Gennadianus 45 and is attributed to Ezra the Priest, to whom the information was *shown*. These Days should probably be considered dated, both due to precession as well as from comparison with other such sequences of Days which are popular to this day across Asia. These Days in the modern Japanese Lunar calendar system are not static, but change each year given the movement and phase of the Moon. In Japanese and Chinese astrological systems an entire year is given to a particular animal and the chart is further refined by understanding in which year the individual was born. While such systems may have once had some equivalent in the West, such as the example below, they have long since vanished from use. For those interested in discovering favourable years, months, and days they are recommended to explore Eastern systems such as the Buddhist *Rokuyo* (六曜) which remain vital and alive.

Beneficial				Month	Malign		
12th	14th	19th	28th	March	30th	8th	
4th	6th	15th	20th	April	3rd	20th	
6th	13th	21st		May	6th	20th	
2nd	11th	15th	21st	June	3rd	18th	
9th	17th	16th	27th	July	6th	20th	
11th	16th	27th		August	2nd	4th	15th
3rd	21st	24th		September	3rd	24th	
2nd	4th	15th		October	3rd	20th	
7th	23rd	27th		November	5th	14th	
5th	13th	25th		December	1st	10th	15th
9th	7th	12th	13th	January	2nd	4th	
4th	7th	12th		February	21st	26th	

Part V: The Catalogue

✠

The Names of the Hours and their Offices

Monday - Hours of the Day				
Planet	**Hour**	**Office**	**Angel**	**Demon**
Moon	1st	For trading & money	Gabriel	Mamonas
Saturn	2nd	**A Bad Hour /** For sickness	Pharsaphael	Skolion
Jupiter	3rd	For opening workshops	Pindoel	Thetidoph
Mars	4th	For binding workshops	Kopiel	Arban
Sun	5th	For selling	Kelekiel	Azan
Venus	6th	For interceding in dealings	Tariel	Memakhth
Mercury	7th	For going on a journey	Mniel	Skamidinos
Moon	8th	For buying / For night work	Ezekiel	Stirphan
Saturn	9th	**Do Nothing /** Restraining	Ioel	Giram
Jupiter	10th	For starting a business	Sinael	Menaktinos
Mars	11th	For preventing luck	Menael	**Mexiphōn**
Sun	12th	For starting a business	Rhokhael	Outolōkh

Part V: The Catalogue

Monday - Hours of the Night					
Planet	Hour	Office	Angel	Demon
Venus	1st	For resting	Aresiel	Nyktidon
Mercury	2nd	For earning a living / profit	Trapedoel	Onistos
Moon	3rd	For working / merchandise	Akinatiel	**Kasieroph**
Saturn	4th	**Do Nothing**	Organiel	**Kysiepotos**
Jupiter	5th	For writing & speaking / hindering	Rhomatiel	**Apophael**
Mars	6th	**Do Nothing** / To restrain & hinder	Selpidon	Nioekh
Sun	7th	For starting plans	Outitom	Entauros
Venus	8th	Do No Work / For resting & planning	Metabiel	Syritor
Mercury	9th	For moving and to stir affairs	Akbael	Phlinaphe
Moon	10th	For early morning planning	Eikoniel	Kyknit
Saturn	11th	**Do No Work**	Genekiel	Kenops
Jupiter	12th	For opening workshops	Krotiel	Sarkidon

Tuesday - Hours of the Day				
Planet	**Hour**	**Office**	**Angel**	**Demon**
Mars	1st	For war and victory	Samouel	Kakiston
Sun	2nd	For taking loot	Iasmel	Lithridon
Venus	3rd	For displays of martial skills	Phrereel	Mailoth
Mercury	4th	For going to war	Eudel	Sarapidie
Moon	5th	For safe travel	Piktoel	**Tartarouēl**[81]
Saturn	6th	**A Dangerous Hour** / Causes conflict	Okael	Kerinoudalos
Jupiter	7th	For appearing before enemies / giving thanks	Gnathael	Klinotios
Mars	8th	For asking for aid	Perganiel	Tyrrytor
Sun	9th	For conquering and looting castles	Gestiel	Plelatan
Venus	10th	For doing mighty deeds	Legmiel	Sythlos
Mercury	11th	For making excuses / standing out	Nakhoel	Osthridie
Moon	12th	Despoiling slain enemies	Oknan	Omitot

---

81 Tartarouēl *or* Karnodēs.

Tuesday - Hours of the Night				
Planet	**Hour**	**Office**	**Angel**	**Demon**
Saturn	1st	**Be careful**	Gorfil	Aprox
Jupiter	2nd	For bringing someone into discredit	Patiel	Skoen
Mars	3rd	For aid and salvation	Partan	Prophai
Sun	4th	**Useless / Do Nothing**	Saltiel	Akhlitol
Venus	5th	For rising in honour	Abael	Hornan
Mercury	6th	For escape or concealment	Stragiel	Khalmoth
Moon	7th	For defeating opponents	Opadouel	Touddeden
Saturn	8th	For marching against enemies	Marniel	Tephra
Jupiter	9th	For concealment	Methniel	Niran
Mars	10th	For praying to God	Stiroel	Rhakiro
Sun	11th	For appearing at war	Ismatiel	Irgotie
Venus	12th	**An Enviable Hour**	Trizioel	Gegaor

Wednesday - Hours of the Day					
Planet	**Hour**	**Office**	**Angel**	**Demon**
Mercury	1st	For invisibility & education	Ouriel	Loutzipher
Moon	2nd	For resting and cheering	Arakel	Goukoumōr
Saturn	3rd	**Do Nothing**	Miemphiel	Eispniryx
Jupiter	4th	For alchemy	Trosiel	Mēdōkit
Mars	5th	For revealing secret things	Khartisel	Ntadadiph
Sun	6th	For finding treasures	Sphykinoel	Skyntogēr
Venus	7th	For dominating a woman	Oulodias	Phnidōtas
Mercury	8th	For influencing a tribunal	Kalbalgiel	Karatan
Moon	9th	For cohabiting with a woman	Skitamiel	Miag
Saturn	10th	**Be Careful**	Tiroel	Gatzar
Jupiter	11th	For all beginnings	Miel	Pnidōr
Mars	12th	**Do Nothing**	Kharakiel	Toiblas

Wednesday - Hours of the Night				
Planet	Hour	Office	Angel	Demon
Sun	1st	For success in discourse	Hydroel	Taxiphōn
Venus	2nd	To begin praying	Sidrel	Ophitan
Mercury	3rd	For dreams	Parapiel	Ablykhos
Moon	4th	For binding spells	Mourouel	Malakis
Saturn	5th	**Do Nothing**	Kourtael	Blemigkh
Jupiter	6th	For harming people	Koupeel	Kheirōn
Mars	7th	For retribution	Peraniel	Ephippas
Sun	8th	For anything	**Satanael**	Orkistaph
Venus	9th	For sending dreams	Katziel	**Loginar**
Mercury	10th	For teaching	Louliel	Pharōs
Moon	11th	For binding spells	**Saltael**	Rhoktat
Saturn	12th	**Do Nothing**	Gabtel	Hopnax

Thursday - Hours of the Day				
Planet	Hour	Office	Angel	Demon
Jupiter	1st	For healing of any living thing	Rhaphael	Meltiphron
Mars	2nd	**Do Nothing**	Perniphel	Hokhlos
Sun	3rd	For appearing before kings	Kisphael	Oueros
Venus	4th	For appearing before a lady	Kaliel	Thaphot
Mercury	5th	For learning rhetoric	Glostas	Tzippat
Moon	6th	For changing residence / For reconciliation	Mnimeel	Amor
Saturn	7th	**Be Careful**	Khariel	Orphor
Jupiter	8th	For blessed beginnings	Skiael	Outaet
Mars	9th	For causing jealousy	Misoel	Ergotas
Sun	10th	For benefitting one's body	Dalphoth	**Azouboul**[82]
Venus	11th	For healing a woman	Khartoel	Aplex
Mercury	12th	For emigrating far away / For craftiness	Kiphar	Sigos

---

82 Possibly a corruption of Belzebuth?

Thursday - Hours of the Night					
PLANET	HOUR	OFFICE	ANGEL	DEMON
Moon	1st	For success	Sitioel	Asmodas
Saturn	2nd	**Useless**	Bokiel	Ouokh
Jupiter	3rd	For every kind of healing	Senoel	Nikokep
Mars	4th	For performing surgery / hunting	Oriator	Kopinos
Sun	5th	For healing kings	Khymeriel	Kaete
Venus	6th	For healing a lady	Orphniel	Lastor
Mercury	7th	For courage before robbers	Kidouel	Epie
Moon	8th	Useful for nocturnal affairs	Gob	Organ
Saturn	9th	**Do Nothing**	Phisnael	Nierier
Jupiter	10th	For anything	Karaael	Oualielos
Mars	11th	For causing hassle	Kondar	Galielior
Sun	12th	For influencing a tribunal and lords	Kispol	Khoukan

Friday - Hours of the Day				
PLANET	HOUR	OFFICE	ANGEL	DEMON
Venus	1st	For causing love and affection	Agathouel	Goulion
Mercury	2nd	For matchmaking	Nidouel	Bizike
Moon	3rd	Good for everything / For selling	Emphiloel	Zorzorath
Saturn	4th	For obstacles of love	Kanikel	Rhaphioph
Jupiter	5th	For gifts / pleasant conversations / decrees	Seliniel	Hermag
Mars	6th	Causing jealousy in love	Karkanpher	Kerinoudalos
Sun	7th	For love	Aniel	Tabaltalis
Venus	8th	For love	Mouriel	Thapnix
Mercury	9th	For secrets / messages / engagements	Tophatiel	Eliasem
Moon	10th	For anything	Skirtouel	Amikh
Saturn	11th	**Do Nothing**	Armoel	Galgidon
Jupiter	12th	For agreements	Otrael	Ephirit

Friday - Hours of the Night					
Planet	**Hour**	**Office**	**Angel**	**Demon**
Mars	1st	For engagements / matchmaking	Talkidonios	Stragiton
Sun	2nd	For binding a couple	Rhoudiel	Antheros
Venus	3rd	For binding someone with love	Thekiel	Pizitor
Mercury	4th	For sending dreams of love	Glykidol	Aprix
Moon	5th	For anything	**Psalmatios**	Niphon
Saturn	6th	For sending dreams of hatred	Stouphouel	Hotrikhos
Jupiter	7th	For anything beneficial	Deaukon	Khimeri
Mars	8th	**Do Nothing**	**Asphrodel**	Moli
Sun	9th	For anything	Tetilol	Kapnithel
Venus	10th	For love	Gorgiel	Takhman
Mercury	11th	For alchemy	Bataaniel	Oukisem
Moon	12th	For restraining love	Polion	Ounipher

Saturday - Hours of the Day				
PLANET	HOUR	OFFICE	ANGEL	DEMON
Saturn	1st	For harming your enemies and striking them with illness	Sakatiel	Klendator
Jupiter	2nd	For causing shipwrecks	Saloel	Kheirim
Mars	3rd	For setting up enchantments	Basael	Spindor
Sun	4th	For making lords fight among themselves	Abael	Keriak
Venus	5th	For making a couple hate each other	Gielmon	Nikem
Mercury	6th	For finding treasure	Rhetael	Moriel
Moon	7th	For speaking with demons	Pelaphiel	Synigeirom
Saturn	8th	For performing basin divination[83]	Samosan	Aphios
Jupiter	9th	For performing skull divination[84]	Pletanix	Thorios
Mars	10th	For causing people to plunge into the sea	Kaponiel	Stelpha
Sun	11th	For making litigants mad at each other	Marmikhael	Kypos
Venus	12th	For fear and enmity	Tekharix	Skar

---

83 Lekanomanteia.

84 Nekromanteia.

Saturday - Hours of the Night				
Planet	**Hour**	**Office**	**Angel**	**Demon**
Mercury	1st	For discovering secret things	Arniel	Tekhar
Moon	2nd	For seeing people long dead	Gilbiel	Akrok
Saturn	3rd	*Hygromanteia*[85]	Golgoel	Argitan
Jupiter	4th	For teaching	Sanipiel	Atomeos
Mars	5th	**Very Malign Hour**	Belarael	Gnotas
Sun	6th	**Do Nothing (Useless Hour)**	Opiael	Merkou
Venus	7th	For gambling	Ophkhinel	Enaritar
Mercury	8th	For restraining every good thing	Patriel	Nioukhan
Moon	9th	**Do Nothing (An hour without virtue)**	Ianiel	Amphou
Saturn	10th	For causing visions	Kondienel	Mankos
Jupiter	11th	For profit	Oxinoel	Moigron
Mars	12th	For causing hassle and enmity	Thanael	Nigrisph

---

85 Binding Demons to water bowls.

Sunday - Hours of the Day					
Planet	**Hour**	**Office**	**Angel**	**Demon**
Sun	1st	**Missing**	Mikhael	Asmodia
Venus	2nd	For gaining the love of lords, great men, and rulers	Arphanael	Ornai
Mercury	3rd	For meeting lords	Perouel	Perrath
Moon	4th	For addressing lords	Iorael	Siledon
Saturn	5th	For preventing encounters	Piel	Sitros
Jupiter	6th	For appearing before lords	Iokhth	Zephar
Mars	7th	**Do Nothing**	Pel	Manier
Sun	8th	For anything regarding lords	Ioran	Osmie
Venus	9th	For anything regarding ladies	Katael	Pnix
Mercury	10th	For making petitions	Bidouel	Gerat
Moon	11th	To begin an address	Bediel	Nesta
Saturn	12th	**Do Nothing**	Sanael	Pelior

Sunday - Hours of the Night				
Planet	**Hour**	**Office**	**Angel**	**Demon**
Jupiter	1st	To speak in aid of friends and allies	Opsiel	Hoistos
Mars	2nd	To prevent an address	Terael	Apios
Sun	3rd	For sending dreams to lords	Lysiel	Negmos
Venus	4th	For sending dreams to ladies	Natouel	Arax
Mercury	5th	**Do Nothing**	Orkiel	Nestriaph
Moon	6th	A good hour for working	Periel	Askinos
Saturn	7th	**Do Nothing**	Iarel	Kinopigos
Jupiter	8th	For the love of lords	Athouel	Araps
Mars	9th	For restraining an opponent	Thamaniel	**Tartarouel**
Sun	10th	For appearing before lords	Bradel	Melmeth
Venus	11th	For appearing before ladies	Klinos	Methridanou
Mercury	12th	For rest	Ion	Phrodainos

✠
NOTES ON THE DAYS

Notes on the Hours of Monday

The catalogues of Names presented contain many inconsistencies and were the impetus for the creation of this text. A reconstruction was attempted, but it is readily admitted now that for such a feat to be truly completed it would require many more data points. MS Monacensis Gr.70 was chosen to be the foundation of this effort as it appears, despite its issues, to be the most complete. The following notes cover a wide range of issues and points of interest, from phonetics, to the Names of Spirits, to placing certain concepts and ideas in their historical context for the reader. Each set of notes progresses through the catalogue of each day sequentially unless there was a specific problem which required a solution before the sequence could be properly established. I refrain from highlighting every single consideration for the sake of brevity. Our week thus begins with the Day of the Moon.

The Angels of Monday appear to be stable enough and so we will begin with the Demons of this Day. Mexiphōn and its variant Mariphōn are variably listed as the Demon of the ninth, tenth, eleventh, and twelfth Hours throughout the manuscripts. This region of the catalogue shows a high level of diversity and inconsistency between sources and our first example of the difficulty in reconstructing the catalogue. Nyktidōn is listed as the Demon of the tenth, eleventh, twelfthth, thirteenth, and fourteenth Hours, as well as being duplicated internally within both MS Atheniensis 1265 and MS Bernardaceus, making it difficult to position with confidence. Onistōs has a similar issue, having various permutations such as Ouistos and Onistros which appear as the Demon of the thirteenth, fourteenth, and fifteenth Hours across the manuscripts. However, the catalogue of Monday found in MS Monacensis Gr.70 contains two major issues which aided in the attempted reconstruction: the first being the duplication of the Demons of the tenth and eleventh Hour, which are listed as Menaktinos and Mekaktinos, respectively. Secondly, the twenty-first Demon is listed as Syritōr-Phlinaphe which is clearly a *doubling up* of the Names of the Demons of the twentieth and twenty-first Hours listed in the other manuscripts separately as Siriton, Sirtōr, Syritōr, and Sēntōr for the Demon of the twentieth Hour, and Phrinaphe, Phloaniphe, Philinoler, and Phylianēre for the Demon of the twenty-first. Thus, with a duplication of Names found at Hours ten and eleven, it became possible to remove the Name of the twelfth Hour, creating an empty entry. Syritōr-Phlinaphe as the twenty-first Hour could then be divided and re-established by comparison to the other manuscripts. Once this was done, the Names of the comparative lists became more coherent and the present list was reconstructed, with Outolōkh in M being moved up from the first Hour of Night to the twelfth Hour of Day where it becomes phonetically comparable to both Ontokhōr and Outolōon, found in A and G respectively. Nyktidōn is then moved up under Outolōkh to become the Demon of the first Hour of Night, where it finds itself comparable with Nyktidōn, Niktidōn and Nyktēdon. Ouistos, or perhaps more accurately Onistos, is moved up to the second Hour of Night, as are all the Names up to the split found at the ninth Hour of Night with Syritor and Phlinaphe.

Once this corrected order has been established, we find the Name of the Demon of the fifth Hour of Night is Androphai; however, it has some alternatives which may be of interest, namely, Androphaēl, Androphagēs and most specifically, Apophaēl. It is also worth noting that the similarities between the Names of the third and fourth Demons of Night are terribly similar in all instances of the reconstructed catalogues. Kasieroph and Kesiepopos have many phonetic similarities which can't be ignored. In fact, there is a great deal of confusion between the entries from the eleventh Demon of Day through to the ninth Demon of Night across all the catalogues for Monday. In particular, Hours three to five of Night are a mixture of Names which ultimately cohere with these three groups, the first being the softer sounding 'ph' group, Kasiereph, Kasior and Kasieroph. This is followed by the 'pop' group: Kysiepotos, Kasioptos, Kysiepetos, and Kēsiepopos, and finally we end with the 'roph' group: Apophaēl, Androphag, Androphagēs, Andropai, and Androphaēl, all of which shares many phonetic similarities with both the 'ph' and the 'pop' groups. This makes any real attempt to tease out which Names are 'correct' fairly difficult.

Notes on the Hours of Tuesday

Once more, despite MS Harleianus 5596 having a massive lacuna between the fourth and thirteenth entries, the Angel Names are stable throughout. We move then directly into our analysis of the Demons, the primary issue of which is found with the Demons of the fifth and sixth Hours of the Day, namely the two Spirits, Tartarouēl and Kerinoudalos. To make matters more complicated, the name of the Demon of the fifth Hour is a replication of that of the Demon of the ninth Hour of night on Sunday. While the order of the lists presented here begin with the Moon to cohere with the Sub-Lunar ontology presented, the original manuscripts begin with the Spirits of the Hours of the Sun and so should perhaps take some precedence in this instance. Given the etymology of the Name Tartarouēl,[86] Tuesday may seem like an unusual Day for this Spirit, however it shares this Martian sympathy with the ninth Hour of Night on the Day of the Sun which falls the Hour of Mars. The only potential alternative Name is found in MS Gennadianus 45, which lists Artagēl. This Name possesses the 'arta' phonetic structure meaning it is more than likely an abbreviated and corrupted instance of the same Name. The Hour of Mars on the Day of the Sun as Tartarus is interesting, yet we find the fifth Hour of the Day of Mars is ruled by the Moon, a far more logical position for this Spirit to reside within. This is all assuming the 'Tartar' phonetic object which forms this Demon's Name possesses the chthonic connotation we are supposing.[87] Given the many other Names which appear throughout the catalogues such as Apophis and Typhon from Egyptian and Greek myth, Asmodius from Judaism, and Lucifer from Christianity, we are dealing with a panoply of intermeshed cultural ideas converging around expressions of chthonic forces. Thus, we find a fascinating set of poles, both with Martian virtue, divided between Day and Night as well as the Hours of the Sun and Moon.

---

86 "'Hell', Greek Ἅιδης (Hadēs), Coptic ⲁⲙⲉⲛⲧⲉ (Amente), refers in popular Egyptian Christianity to the underworld. Prior to the resurrection of Jesus, nearly all the human dead were confined in hell, but after his resurrection, only the evil were kept there, while the righteous were taken to Paradise (paradeisos) to await final judgement. Hell is overseen by angels who punish sinners, whose ruler is known as Temeluchus or Tartaruchus ("ruler of Tartarus"), and is also the place to which the fallen angels, or demons, are confined as punishment. There is often a conflation between the angels of hell and the demons, and thus the ruler of hell and the Devil. The deepest and most terrible part of hell is referred to as Tartarus (Τάρταρος). Hell may also be referred to as the *abyss, a term originally referring to the primordial waters below the earth." From Korshi Dosoo, & Markéta Preininger, eds, *Papyri Copticae Magicae: Coptic Magical Texts* Volume 1: Formularies. (Berlin: de Gruyter, 2023) p. 478.

87 Although this may have no relevance to this study, it should be noted that in 1714 a recension of Hygromanteia (MS Petropolitanus Academicus), was in the possession of a Russian monk of the monastery of Saint Nicolaus, Moscow, who migrated to the city of Kazan, Tatarstan. Could there be a chance, however slim, that this Spirit is the genius loci of this country as opposed to being a reference to the Greek Tartarus? Probably not, but interesting regardless.

There is a broad consensus among the manuscripts of Tuesday despite the usual variations in spelling, with even MS Bernardaceus, the most corrupt, in agreement. The problem we find is that the Harleianus 5596 manuscript can't help us due to the Names of the fourth to thirteenth Hours being lost or unrecorded. What's more, MS Atheniensis 1265 frustratingly lists the Names of the Demons of the fifth, sixth, and seventh Hours as Kernoudēs, Kerinoude and Kyienotēs, all of which are more than likely duplicates of the same Name. Keridonal and Kerinoudalos, the Names of the Demons of the sixth Hour are painfully similar to these Names, suggesting that the MS Gennadianus 45 and MS Monacenis Gr.70 catalogues have these Names in the correct positions. After careful consideration this seems to be one of the few instances where the Bernardaceus catalogue comes in useful. As with the duplication of the tenth Demon of the Moon, Menaktino, in the MS Monacensis Gr.70 catalogue, the Demons of the ninth and tenth, the thirteenth and fifteenth, and the eighteenth and nineteenth Hours of Tuesday in Bernardaceus catalogue are duplicates. Again, this was done by examining the various phonetic structures of each Name. It is very safe to conclude that MS Bernardaceus is thoroughly corrupt given the number of duplications, but what it does is highlight where the error may have crept in. This is surely at the fifth Hour, as each Name from this entry to the twenty-second has been moved up in the list by one position. This must have occurred when, for whatever reason, the Name of the fifth Hour was found missing or skipped by accident, consequently resulting in a corrupted list having to duplicate entries to make up for the omission. While MS Atheniensis 1265 definitely possesses a duplicate of the fifth Name of the Hour, this Name is not Tartarouēl, but Kernoudēs. Making things even more complicated still, we find that many Names of Spirits, both Angels and Demons, were included in the 'Short Lists' of various manuscripts of *Hygromanteia* to be used in the conjurations of the Planets as their Rulers, and that the overwhelming majority, five from a total of seven sources, all list Tartarouēl as the principal Demon of the Moon.

This unfortunately leaves us in the situation where we have to make a choice between a Name which has obviously been imported from another list as a means to fill an empty entry within the catalogue, or a highly suspect duplication which shares far too many phonetic objects to be satisfactorily considered a unique Name. Ultimately the reader is left to their own conclusions.

Notes on the Hours of Wednesday

There is not much to comment on with this catalogue save the choice to change the Name of the Angel of the eighth Hour of the Night from Santaēl as found in MS Monacensis Gr.70 to the far more likely Satanaēl as found in MS Harleianus 5596, given that MS Gennadianus 45 lists the name as Sataēl. This should hopefully highlight something of the Sublunary nature of the 'Angels'[88] we are engaging with in these manuscripts.[89] This entry is also somewhat unusual in that it is one of only five instances where, *"Anything"* is given as the office of a Spirit. These particular Spirits and the astrological conditions under which they operate must be considered in some way significant and perhaps diametrically opposed to instances where we are informed to "Do Nothing". On examination we find:

Eighth Hour of Night - Wednesday - Hour of the Sun / Satanael - Orkistaph
Tenth Hour of Night - Thursday - Hour of Jupiter / Karaael - Oualielos
Tenth Hour of Day - Friday - Hour of the Moon / Skirtouel - Amikh
Fifth Hour of Night - Friday - Hour of the Moon / Psalmatios - Niphon
Ninth Hour of Night - Friday - Hour of the Sun / Tetilol - Kapnithel

Astrologically minded readers will notice that all of these permutations of Day and Hour involve the non-Malefic Planets, the most common being Venus, the Lesser Benefic which, with three entries of this type, immediately sets it apart, not to mention that it is the only example in the entire catalogue where Spirits listed under the Hours of the Day are given the office of *Anything*.

To conclude Wednesday, there is a single entry where MS Monacensis Gr.70 stands out when compared with the other manuscripts, all of which list the Demon of the 9th hour of the Night as Loginar. MS Monacensis Gr.70 provides Loginaph, which is admittedly a minor adaptation. Given the consensus across the manuscripts the Name here was altered.

---

88 For more on this Spirit see the Appendix: Satanael.
89 Harry E. Gaylord, 'How Satanael lost his "el"', *Journal of Jewish Studies*, 33, no. 1-2, (1982) 303-309: "Le diable garde les lieux inferieurs, ils'etait fait Satan quand ilavait fui du ciel, car son nom etait Satanael".

Notes on the Hours of Thursday

Raphael may seem out of place as the spirit *par excellence* of Thursday, although given that there is already ambiguity as to a 'correct' Planetary correspondence with this Archangel, specifically with his attention being divided between Mercury and the Sun.[90] As we already have such a plurality of authority constellating about this one Spirit, it shouldn't be such a stretch to allow this Spirit governance over the Planet Jupiter as well. Marathakis points out in his translation of *Hygromanteia*[91] that Raphael is similarly attested as the Spirit of Jupiter in *Picatrix*, where we find the following invocation:

> O RAFAEL the King. The Authorizer of **Jupiter**, the happy, the complete, the whole, the good, with the good taste, the respectable, the smart, the far away from contamination and bad sayings, I call you with all your names, in Arabic MUSHTARY, in Persian BARGEES, in Barbarian HURMUZ, in Greek ZAWISH, and in Indian WAHSAFT. In the Name of the Upper Creators and Gods and Blessings, I ask you to do for me so and so.[92]

Pigeonholes are not the best places to store Spirits; they have a habit of breaking out of them. Perhaps it would be far better to instead contemplate Spirits as having a spectrum of *modalities*; Raphael then is of such an authority among the Spirits that he may wield authority over various planetary virtues and be employed in a multiplicity of forms. We had best avoid the desire to apply modern mechanical thinking to our categorisations, instead embracing that different Spirits find different modes of expression over history and from culture to culture. Perhaps we can equally apply this to the above Spirit, Tartarouēl.

The first attempted correction in this catalogue is minor, being a change to the seventh Angel of the Day found in MS Monacensis Gr.70, Kalriel. This Name is too phonetically similar to the fourth Angel of the Day, Kaliel, and in comparison it seems prudent to drop the superfluous 'l'.

---

90 See, for example, the works of Averroes, Ibn Ezra, Pietro d'Abano (1303), and the *Heptameron* of Pseudo-d'Abano (1559).

91 Marathakis, p. 69.

92 Hashem Atallah, trans. & William Kiesel, ed. *Picatrix: Ghayat Al-Hakim: The Goal of the Wise*, vol. 1 (Seattle: Ouroboros Press, 2002) p.74.

The eighth Angel of the Day also poses something of an issue, mostly due to MS Harleianus 45 once more possessing lacunae which prevent us from performing a more accurate comparison. Both MS Gennadianus 45 and MS Monacensis Gr.70 list Skiael, whereas MS Atheniensis 1265 and Bernardaceus list Omeel or Omiel, which are phonetically unrelated to the point they are almost certainly different Names. Unfortunately, the adjacent entries provide us with little to go on, save that the 'Sk' phonetic object may have been duplicated in the seventh entry in Gennadius as Skhariel. Alternatively, perhaps it was this phonic which was mistakenly duplicated in the creation of the Name Skiael found in the eighth entry of both G and M, and it was Omiel which was the original entry. Without a fifth comparative point this will unfortunately remain too ambiguous to make a concrete conclusion. As the Name Skiael is phonetically distinct enough, it remained in the presented catalogue, as posing an alternative would have been too tentative.

Both the fourteenth and fifteenth entries, Bokiel and Senoel, remain as they are presented in MS Monacensis Gr.70; despite the alternative spellings in the comparative catalogues there are just enough phonetic similarities for them to remain unchanged. However, the twentieth entry, Goth, was unique in its spelling as found in M, and while I am fairly sure its position in the catalogue is solid, the alternative spellings in different positions, namely the Angel of the sixth Hour of Night in A, of the eighth Hour of Night in G, and of the 7th Hour of Night in B, all of which list the Name of this Spirit as Gob(el), was enough to warrant its alteration. Gob, the King of the Gnomes, will be familiar to those of you interested in the Elemental Kings as well as the works of Paracelsus and the Comte de Gabalis. If we assume that an entry similar to Gob/Goth/Gobel was present in the lacuna of the Angel of the ninth Hour of Night in MS Harleianus 45, which otherwise has no phonetically similar entry, we find the potential Planetary Hours of this Spirit being Venusian, Mercurial, Lunar, or Saturnian. The Elemental King Gob would perhaps be quite comfortable in the hour of Saturn, as he rules under Capricorn in the South which is domicile to the dour Wanderer. Given further context, the geographical distances and centuries of time between the penning of these Names, as well as the etymological root of Gob coming from the old French *Gobelin*, Medieval Latin *Gobelinus*, which probably arrived from the German *Kobold* and the Greek *Kobalos*, mean it is safe to say this entry in the catalogue is nothing more than a homonym.

Finally, all the entries in all five manuscripts for the Angels between the eighth and twelfth Hours of Night are highly divergent, with multiple lacunae. As a result, no single conclusive set of Names can be repaired and the MS Monacensis Gr.70 catalogue was simply followed for consistency. Examples of this divergence are the Names of the Angels of the eleventh Hour of Night, which from H, A, G, M and B respectively are listed as, Kondarke, Kipol, Kalidad, Kondar, and Kotael. Their only phonetic consistency is the initial 'K', and unfortunately the adjacent Names, save Kispol as the Angel of the twelfth Hour of Night in M, don't offer much for us to reconstruct.

Moving on to the Demons of the Day and Night of this, the Day of Jupiter: while the Name listed above is based on the most common variants across the manuscripts, MS Atheniensis 1265 interestingly lists the first Demon of the Day under Raphael as Typhonbon. While the 'ph' phonic is consistent throughout, it is otherwise far too divergent and upon inspecting the list we find that Meliphon is indeed present, but has somehow been moved from being the Angel of the first Hour of Day, to being that of the twelfth Hour of Night. It is always interesting to note when mythological Names appear, in this case the issue seems to have arisen from the Names of the twelfth Demon of Night being mostly absent, with only two out of five surviving examples, both of which are radically different. The first is found in A, which lists the Name as Lior, the second is in M, our foundational catalogue, which lists Khoukan. Neither have any apparent proximate duplications or similar phonetic structures with other Names in any catalogue. A secondary set of evidence for the Names of the last five Hours of the catalogues of the Demons of Thursday is found from the sixth Hour of Night where the Names begin to become noticeably misordered, as can be seen with the Names Epios / Epie, Nierier / Nieriel, Organ / Orgau and Oualielo / Ouanleilos. The error seems to constellate around the lacuna for the ninth Hour of Night found in A.

We see many examples where Names tend to lose or gain a letter in similar patterns across the various manuscripts. One such example is the dropping of an initial consonant or consonant pair, an example being the Demon of the third Hour of Wednesday, which is listed in H, A, G, M, and B as Eistierix, Ispnyrix, Hypnirix, Eispniryx, and Ipnerix, respectively. Here we can see how, despite the phonetic structures of all the Names remaining consistent, there is still a significant drift. We see the Name listed under G has maintained its initial 'H' phonic before the vowel, although the specific case of the English H being used by Marathakis is to indicate an aspiration present at the beginning of the Name and it shouldn't be confused with the actual English letter. We see this same process when we look at the Demon of the second Hour of Night on Wednesday which is listed as Hophetes, whereas all its equivalents drop the initial 'H' to form Names such as Ophitan and Ophitas. The same thing occurs in the very same catalogue when we see A list Hopnax, the twelfth Demon of Night, whereas A, G, and B list Opnax, Opnaz, and Apnax. While vowels make such switches, consonants tend to do this more frequently, especially letters with similar phonemes. For this reason, Hokhlos, while being the outlier across the catalogues, was selected because it perhaps preserves the initial aspirated 'H' sound which all the other extant examples have since lost.

Next we come to the Demon of the tenth Hour of the Day, Azouboul, which is awfully close to the various spellings of Berzeboul, Berzebeoul, and Beelzebuth; although reconstructing it as such may be a stretch, there are many examples of Spirit Names across these catalogues which have either lost their initial consonant sound, had the first vowel sound of their Name changed slightly, or both. It has remained with its original spelling in the catalogue presented above and the reader is invited to form their own opinion on the matter. If the tenth Hour of Thursday is ruled by the Sun and Belzebuth, then the first Hour of Night on that same day is ruled by Asmodas and the Moon, which harkens back to our previous analysis of the North. Comparing the Name with the other manuscripts we find H and G have very similar phonetic objects, whereas A and B both share a rather different Name which is clearly of a separate origin, namely Okokes and Akokeph, both of which seem to be aliases of the subsequent Hour's Demon, Ouokh. Again we are faced with a similar issue of duplication across the Days as that we have already mentioned with the likes of Tartaroēl. Given that Raphael is described as the Angel that frustrates Asmodeus in both the second-century BCE Book of Tobit as well as the *Testament of Solomon*, there really is no question as to the solidity of this position within the list. Perhaps then, instead of attempting to force the matter we should instead accept that this very high-ranking superior Spirit has two modalities, one Lunar during the first Hour of Night on a Thursday, the other Solar which is expressed during the first Hour of the Day of the Sun.

Notes on the Hours of Friday

Beginning with the Angel of the first Hour of the Day we find Agathouel. Agath(a) comes from the Greek *Agathos*, a word meaning *Good* or *Honourable*. This Name is exceptionally interesting given the importance throughout the *Greek Magical Papyri* of the *Agathos Daimon* (ἀγαθός δαίμων), the *Good Genius*, who can be found throughout Graeco-Egyptian magical practices as well as being a common God of the Household in classical Greek religion, often being invoked during a banquet or having libations poured for them upon completion of a meal. This Spirit is the male partner of Tyche, or Fortune, both of whom are often depicted as serpents. The *Agathos Daimon* is described as both a Guide and as an Intermediary, interceding with the Gods on behalf of the sorcerer-priest, an assistant in much the same way, if not identical to, the contemporary practice of developing a relationship with an Intermediary as found within a grimoire such as the *Grimorium Verum* or *Liber Officiorum Spirituum*.[93]

Agatha of Sicily (231-251 AD), a young virgin martyr and patron saint of breasts and bakers, possessing certain virtues which calm the anger of Mt Etna, prison of Typhon as well as the location of the forges of Hephaestus, is another potential root of the Name. Given this thread it may be possible, even if at a stretch, to consider the Name of the Olympic Spirit of Venus, *Hagith*, as a possible linguistic evolution of *Agatha*, although this remains highly speculative.

The spelling of the Angel of the third Hour, Emphiloel, was selected from MS Gennadianus 45, as the initial vowel 'E' is more common than 'A'. The 'iloel' suffix is also more common, with three examples compared to cases of 'inoel'.

The Angel of the seventh Hour of Day, Aniel, being the Spirit of the Planetary forces of Venus on the Day of the Sun is our well known and known *Anael*, as found as the Angelic ruler of Friday in the *Heptameron* as well as the Spirit conjured for the experiment of the Mirror given in the *Grimorium Verum*.[94] Both A and B lack Aniel, listing Kaniel and Mouke. Kaniel is definitely a permutation of her alias, Haniel. As for Mouke, this is simply a continuation of the many mistakes found in B, specifically a duplicate entry copied from the row below, an issue we have seen many times now where a missing Name is simply replaced with the Name of the Spirit in the subsequent Hour, often spelt identically.

---

93 Those intermediaries being Scirlin / Syrach, and Tantavalerion, respectively.
94 Peterson, *Grimorium Verum*, pp.75-77.

The fourth Angel of Night is Glykidol, perhaps the Serpent God Glykon of the Macedonians and later Romans. Said to be the reincarnation of Asclepius, this God aids in fertility and protects from plague. This God was popular enough to be minted on coins under Philip II in the third century CE.

The fifth Angel of Night is Psalmatios, important as the Spirit of the Moon on the Day of Venus, a permutation which makes it one of the few Spirits, alongside its Demon, Niphron, to have the Office over "Anything". While this Name may be an aptronym stemming from the collection of Biblical hymns, if we follow the etymology we find the Greek, *psalmos*, meaning, 'to pluck the strings of a harp'. Other Spirits are said to reside within or guard over religious texts, an example being the Sar Torah, the Prince of the Torah, evoked in Jewish theurgical practice with the goal of attaining direct knowledge from the Divine. This form of Jewish esotericism draws from an anthology of Biblical texts, which includes the Psalms.

Asphrodēl, the eighth Angel of the Night, being the third Spirit of Mars on the Day of Venus, creates conditions which the scribes concluded to be fruitless, listing the office as "Do Nothing", while the previous two entries, namely the Spirits of the sixth Hour of the Day and the Spirits of the first Hour of Night are listed as having the offices of causing jealousy in love and aiding in engagements and matchmaking. This Name is listed in M as *Asphodēl*, while all other instances within the catalogues possess the 'r' phonic. In Greek myth the *Asphodel*[95] Meadow of Hades is an aerial region of the Underworld between the Earth and Moon connected via the river Styx, and so, as with Tartarouēl, we find another example of a Spirit named after a region of the Greek Underworld. This Name also has some similarities to Asmodas / Asmodai and may be another modality of this powerful Spirit, much like the previously mentioned *Asmodel* found in the work of Agrippa and associated with Taurus. As the 'ph' (φ) phonic is being used across these entries of the manuscripts it may simply be that this is a unique Spirit with only a superficial similarity, but as in each case the changing of a φ to a Mu (μ) is all that is necessary for the Name to be far more similar. The office of "Do Nothing" in this case may be a prudish countermeasure by the scribe who was uncomfortable with the notion of the creation of a sexually charged talisman with both Martian and Venusian qualities, or it may be perhaps a perceived cancelling out of Planetary dignities.

---

95 Asphodelus of the family Asphodelaceae, is a perennially flowering plant found about the Mediterranean, Northern Africa, and Near East.

Finally, the ninth Angel of Night is clearly suffering from a case of a 't' being switched out for a 'p', and as the remainder of the Name, '-etilol', is prevalent, the spelling as found in H was selected as the clearest reading.

Moving on to the Demons of Friday, we begin with Bizike, the Demon of the second Hour of Day which was selected from A due to the commonality of the vowels, of which there are three out of five examples. This Name has a surprising variation in this one vowel, being 'ou', 'i', or 'e' respectively. There is also a strong consistency with the phonetic 'k' as well as another three out of five examples of the final 'e' sound. Finally, we see an example of a 'z' and 'x' swap here in Bernardaceus which lists the Name as Bixike. This 'z' and 'x' switch happens fairly frequently but as this is only one example and it happens to be in B which is highly untrustworthy, it wasn't considered further. *Bizike* is then the most likely reconstruction. Other examples of this same switch within the Friday catalogue are the Demon of the eighth Hour of the Day, Thapnix, spelled *Thapniz* in G, followed by the Demon of the third Hour of Night, Pizitor, which is spelled Pixitor in A. The subsequent Demon, Aprix is spelled *Apiz* and is also found in G.

There remains little to discuss in this specific catalogue, making the Names of the Demons of Friday one of the most stable. The spelling *Moli*, the eigth Demon of the Night was selected from A due to an overall phonetic consistency, with the initial vowel being an 'O' and the lack of the final 'n' sound only existing in H with any certainty. The tenth Demon of Night, Takhman, despite the lacunae in H, is unusual as it is one of only a handful of examples of a Name with complete consistency throughout all five manuscripts. Finally, the spelling of Ounipher for the twelfth Demon of Night was selected from G as the first 'r' in '-phrer' can be seen to be superfluous after comparison with the other Names.

Notes on the Hours of Saturday

While Saturday contains some of the most important Spirits in the entire catalogue, it is also the most highly corrupted. Saturday is of particular note due to a group of unique offices it contains which will have their own chapter below focusing on several core magical techniques described within *The Magical Treatise of Solomon*. These techniques include *Lekanomanteia*, *Nekromanteia*, as well as the namesake of this collection of manuscripts, *Hygromanteia*. Despite the obvious Jewish influence of the Sabbath, Saturn's

Day is decidedly the day for beginning the Work of this grimoire,[96] listing Spirits which aid us in forming bonds with allies that can specifically aid us in our further explorations of sorcery.

Despite H having lacunae at the second Hour of Night and again from the sixth through the twelfth, the Names as presented appear to only have mild superficial differences. Without exception, each Name from M was faithfully copied, making it an impressively stable Name list. Spirits with familiar Names include Moriel, Skar, and Argitan/Aritan.

Turning to the Names of the Angels of Day and Night we find a minor issue arises with a comparison of the Names of the Angels of the fifth Hour of Day in both A and B, which list *Sielkin / Selieel*, in contrast to the other three catalogues listing *Giel / Gielmon*. Neither of these Names has alternatives, and while both possess the 'ie(l)' phonic object, one of the most common suffixes attributed to Angels, after some thought I am sure this is a sequence of linear corruptions between A and B which appear prevalent throughout this analysis. Thus we find *Giel* to *Gielmon* in H, G and M, and *Sielkin* to *Selieel* between A and the much later B. The next inconsistency presented becomes a significant issue at the eighth and ninth Hours of Day where we see another set of problems arise in A and B, this time as an issue between the order of the Names *Samosan* and *Plentanix*. The ninth Hour also contains three further anomalies: first that the Name *Pletanix* is absent from MS Gennadianus 45. Next, MS Atheniensis 1265 lists *Kismosan* as the ninth Angel of the Day which only has an equivalent in MS Bernardaceus under the Name *Kyssamomael*. As with the previous Names, *Sielkin* and *Selieel*, they at first seem to have no equivalents in any of the other three manuscripts; however, both Names can be seen to be continuing the theme of corruption found between A and B. Phonetically both *Kismosan* and *Kyssamomael* both contain 'S(a)mo(san)', with the entry in B adding an additional angelic '-ael' suffix common to Angel Names. Finally, we find Katones listed in G at the ninth Hour, which appears to be a variant of Kaponiel found in every catalogue except MS Monacensis Gr.70, our baseline document.

At this stage it serves to take a step back to look at the larger picture, much as we had to do in our reconstruction of the Names of the Demons of Tuesday. MS Harleianus 5596 once more suffers from a long sequence of lacunae, with the Angels of the seventh to the twelfth Hours of Night missing. We also find that both G and M have duplicates of Pitriel that

---

96 While Friday is singled out as the "day of preparation". See Skinner & Rankine, *The Veritable Key of Solomon*, p. 58.

are found as the second and eighth Angels of Night. When compared, there seems to be a sequence issue between these Angels in the second Hour of Night position and that of the third Hour of Night, *Golgoel*, who is absent from both MS Atheniensis 1265 and MS Bernardaceus. The fourth Angel of Night, however, *Sanipiel*, is stable across the catalogues, providing us a solid point across the board from which we can begin to attempt a reconstruction. Below this point we find that, if we remove the duplication of Patriel as the eighth Angel of Night and move the ninth, tenth and eleventh Angels up a slot each, MS Monacensis Gr.70 immediately coheres better with the other lists, leaving us with three major issues to solve. Firstly, there is no apparent equivalent of *Kaponiel* found in M, secondly, we are forced to remove *Golgoel* from the list as it has no other location to inhabit, and thirdly, the eleventh Hour of Night is left empty, leaving us with a list which remains broken.

Due to the complexity of corruption in this catalogue it is best to have a visual aide to help in understanding how this reconstruction was accomplished. Below you will find a comparative colour-coded table which will allow the reader to understand how this reconstruction was performed. Names highlighted in bold red italics within parentheses may have been added by the scribe at some point within the document's history as a means to fix the list. It is highly unlikely any one scribe would have had any comparative lists from which to draw. Having access to the work of Marathakis and Greenfield has been a blessing for which I am forever grateful. Names in bold red are duplicates. The colour-coding simply expresses where consistent Names fall within the manuscripts for ease of sight and understanding. Arrows indicate where each Name has been moved or entered into an empty location. The final, completed chart will make this simple to understand. A dash simply means there is a lacuna. *Nagiel*, the ninth Angel of Night as found in G is the only Spirit presented which has no known equivalent. If only H didn't have so many missing entries, we would have had another point of comparison with which this reconstruction would possibly have been far easier.

UNEDITED COMPARATIVE 1			
ANGELS OF ♄			
Hrs of Day/ Night	Harleianus	Atheniensis 1265	Gennadianus
1	Sakipiel	Sakatiel	Sakapiel
2	Saliel	Saloel	Saloel
3	Besael	Thebael	Besael
4	Abael	Abaeli	Abael
5	Giel	*(Sielkin)*	Gielmon
6	Rhetael	Rhetael	Rhetael
7	Pelaphiel	Pelaphiel	Pelaphiel
8	Samosan	Plenanix	Samosan
9	Platanix	*(Kismosan)*	Katones
10	Kapounel	Kaponiel	Marnikhael
11	Marnikhael	Mesnikhael	Ntekhariz
12	Altekharix	Tekharyx	Arniel
1	Arniel	Arniel	Gerbiel
2	Berbiel	Gilbiel	**Petreel**
3	Golgiel	**Tetriel**	Gorgoel
4	Sanipiel	Sanypiel	Skyepika
5	Bekharael	Berael	Belaratat
6	Apiael	Opiael	Optael
7	-	Ophtiel	Ophkhinel
8	-	Ianouel	**Patriel**
9	-	Koudrouel	*(Nagiel)*
10	-	Ouxynoel	Kondiroel
11	-	**Banael**	Oxioel
12	-	Banael	Anael

UNEDITED COMPARATIVE 2

Angels of ♄

Hrs of Day/Night	Monacensis	Bernardaceus
1	Sabapiel	Sakatiel
2	Saloel	Saloel
3	Besael	Thebael
4	Abael	-
5	Gielmon	*(Selieel)*
6	Rhetael	Rhatael
7	Pelaphiel	Pelaphiel
8	Samosan	Pletaniel
9	Pletanix	*(Kyssamomael)*
10	Marmikhael	Kaponiel
11	Ntekharigx	Maphekhlee
12	Arkiel	Tekharer
1	Geabiel	Arniel
2	**Pitriel**	Gelbiel
3	Golgoel	**Tetriel**
4	Sanipiel	Sknipiel
5	Belarael	Beriel
6	Opiael	Opiakel
7	Ophkhinel	Ophriel
8	**Patriel**	Iannouel
9	Ianiel	Koudrouel
10	Kondienel	Oxinoel
11	Ouxounouel	Bannael
12	Thanael	-

We see that Tetriel/Petreel/Pitriel/Tetriel, in the second and third Hours of Night either replace Golgiel entirely in A and B or are forced into the second Hour between Geabiel and Golgoel creating the displacement in the sequence above Sanipiel. This inclusion forced the removal of

Kaponiel from M. By removing Pitriel from the second and third Hours we see the Names from the ninth of Day to the first of Night in G *fall* down a position. Removing the superfluous Kismosan and Kyssamomael from A and B *drops* Plenanix/Pletaniel in the same way. Suddenly our list looks a whole lot smoother.

ANNOTATED COMPARATIVE 1		
Hrs of Day/Night	**Harleianus**	**Atheniensis 1265**
1	Sakipiel	Sakatiel
2	Saliel	Saloel
3	Besael	Thebael
4	Abael	Abaeli
5	Giel	(Sielkin)
6	Rhetael	Rhetael
7	Pelaphiel	Pelaphiel
8	Samosan →	Plenanix ↓
9	Platanix →	(Kismosan)
10	Kapounel	Kaponiel
11	Marnikhael	Mesnikhael
12	Altekharix	Tekharyx
1	Arniel	Arniel
2	Berbiel	Gilbiel
3	Golgiel	Tetriel
4	Sanipiel	Sanypiel
5	Bekharael	Berael
6	Apiael	Opiael
7	-	← Ophtiel
8	Patriel*	Ianouel ↓
9	-	Koudrouel ↓
10	-	Ouxynoel ↓
11	-	Banael
12	-	← Banael

Part V: The Catalogue

Hrs of Day/Night	Gennadianus	Monacensis	Bernardaceus
ANNOTATED COMPARATIVE 2			
1	Sakapiel	Sabapiel	Sakatiel
2	Saloel	Saloel	Saloel
3	Besael	Besael	Thebael
4	Abael	Abael	-
5	← Gielmon	Gielmon →	(Selieel)
6	Rhetael	Rhetael	Rhatael
7	Pelaphiel	Pelaphiel	Pelaphiel
8	Samosan	Samosan →	Pletaniel ↓
9	Katones ↓	Pletanix →	*(Kyssamomael)*
10	Marnikhael ↓	-	← Kaponiel
11	Ntekhariz ↓	Marmikhael	Maphekhlee
12	Arniel ↓	Tekharix	Tekharer
1	Gerbiel ↓	Arniel	Arniel
2	~~Petreel~~	-	← Gelbiel
3	Gorgoel	Golgoel	Tetriel
4	~~Skyepika~~	Sanipiel	Sknipiel
5	Belaratat	Belarael	Beriel
6	Optael	Opiael	Opiakel
7	Ophkhinel	Ophkhinel	Ophriel
8	← **Patriel**	**Patriel** →	Iannouel ↓
9	~~Nagiel~~	← Ianiel	Koudrouel ↓
10	Kondiroel	Kondienel	Oxinoel ↓
11	Oxioel	Oxinoel	Bannael ↓
12	Anael	Thanael	-

A possesses a duplication of Banael, which duplications, as we have seen, are usually added above the proper entry. With its removal the eighth through tenth Names of Night *fall* a position. The exact same can easily be done in B with Names from Iannouel through Bannael simply *falling* down a single position to fill the lacuna in the twelfth Hour. Patriel as the Name of the eighth Angel of Night fills the spaces which open in these lists, and with the removal of Nagiel, replacing it with Ianiel, we find the catalogues restored, perhaps to something closer to the original form.

RECONSTRUCTED COMPARATIVE 1		
Hrs of Day/Night	Harleianus	Atheniensis 1265
1	Sakipiel	Sakatiel
2	Saliel	Saloel
3	Besael	Thebael
4	Abael	Abaeli
5	Giel	**Gielmon**
6	Rhetael	Rhetael
7	Pelaphiel	Pelaphiel
8	Samosan	**Samosan**
9	Platanix	**Plenanix**
10	Kapounel	Kaponiel
11	Marnikhael	Mesnikhael
12	Altekharix	Tekharyx
1	Arniel	Arniel
2	Berbiel	Gilbiel
3	Golgiel	Golgoel
4	Sanipiel	Sanypiel
5	Bekharael	Berael
6	Apiael	Opiael
7	Ophkhinel	Ophtiel
8	Patriel	Patriel
9	Ianiel	Ianouel
10	Kondienel	**Koudrouel**
11	Oxinoel	**Ouxynoel**
12	Thanael	Banael

Hrs of Day/Night	RECONSTRUCTED COMPARATIVE 2		
	Gennadianus	**Monacensis**	**Bernardaceus**
1	Sakapiel	Sabapiel	Sakatiel
2	Saloel	Saloel	Saloel
3	Besael	Besael	Thebael
4	Abael	Abael	**Abael**
5	Gielmon	Gielmon	**Gielmon**
6	Rhetael	Rhetael	Rhatael
7	Pelaphiel	Pelaphiel	Pelaphiel
8	Samosan	Samosan	**Samosan**
9	**Pletanix**	Pletanix	**Pletanix**
10	**Katones**	Kaponiel	Kaponiel
11	**Marnikhael**	Marmikhael	Maphekhlee
12	**Ntekhariz**	Tekharix	Tekharer
1	**Arniel**	Arniel	Arniel
2	**Gerbiel**	Gilbiel	Gelbiel
3	Gorgoel	Golgoel	**Golgoel**
4	Skyepika	Sanipiel	Sknipiel
5	Belaratat	Belarael	Beriel
6	Optael	Opiael	Opiakel
7	Ophkhinel	Ophkhinel	Ophriel
8	Patriel	Patriel	**Patriel**
9	**Ianiel**	Ianiel	**Iannouel**
10	Kondiroel	Kondienel	**Koudrouel**
11	Oxioel	Oxinoel	Oxinoel
12	Anael	Thanael	Bannael

Despite this catalogue posing the single most challenging reconstruction of all the Days of the week presented in this text, with multiple sequential issues, duplicates, mysterious extras, and lacunae, once its reconstruction is completed we find one of the most consistent sets of Names available.

As for the origins of Nagiel, we are at a loss. Perhaps it was once an important Name in the lists which predated our current set; perhaps it was hastily invented by a scribe or copyist, or conjured via some lost means of isopsephy or magical operation.

Note on the Hours of Sunday

The most startling issue we are immediately presented with concerning the Hours of the Sun is that in every single extant version of the available manuscripts the description of the office of the first Hour of the Sun is missing. Despite the original words being long lost we needn't worry, as with the first Hour of every day, the virtue of the Planet which rules is considered at its zenith, and so we find that the description of the first Hour of each Day suggests the creation of a talisman which epitomises these qualities. Thus the first Hour of the Day of Mars is for securing Victory at War, the first Hour of the Day of Venus secures Love, and the first Hour of the Day of Saturn is used to Destroy one's enemies. Thus, for the Sun, the centre of the Solar system and which all others orbit, we gain access to the virtues of Authority, Dignity, Vitality, and Lordship, for casting light upon darkness, and for the revealing of treasures and secrets.

The Angel Names listed are thankfully stable and required no reconstruction or even analysis. The list of the Demons is also highly stable save for the abovementioned potential duplication of the Demon of the ninth Hour of Night, Tartarouel. Other Demons of note within the list include another example of Asmodai, whom we have already discussed at length, as well as Ornias, both of whom are familiar to us from the *Testament of Solomon*. Zephar, listed as the Demon of the sixth Hour of the Day, may be related to the eighteenth Spirit found in Weyer's *Pseudomonarchia Daemonum*,[97] Zepar, although it is just as likely we are dealing with an adaptation of the Greek word, 'Zephyr', the Name of the West Wind. We also find Sitros in the Hour above Zephar, whose Name is passingly similar to Sitri, also present within Weyer, although such a thread is extremely tenuous at best. The remainder of the catalogue of the Sun has some examples of letter switching and positions being swapped; however, the layout of the list found in M appears stable and without need for correction.

---

97 Weyer, Johann. *Pseudomonarchia Daemonum*. trans. by Paul Summers Young (Hanover: Black Letter Press, 2023)

✠
Seven Hours of Saturn and the Sorcery of the Hygromanteia

Lists detailing the rulers of the Hours exist in documents that far predate the *Magical Treatise*, such as those found in PGM IV. 1596-1715 and PGM VII. 862-918, namely the rulers of the unequal Hours of Day and Night found in the 'Consecration of the Twelve Faces of Helios' and the 'Lunar Spell of Klaudianos', respectively. I would posit, then, that this further adds to the argument that, despite the overtly Christian gloss which has been applied to the categories of the Spirits of the Hours found in the *Magical Treatise*, we are dealing with Spirits which predate dualistic Christian terminologies.[98]

Saturn is a uniquely interesting day given the highly specified offices of fourteen of its Spirits. These offices include, *Speaking with Demons, Lekanomanteia, Nekromanteia,* Discovering Secrets, Seeing People Long Dead, *Hygromanteia* and Causing Visions. Speaking with Demons stands out as a particularly interesting office, given that we are already dealing with these Spirits of the Air found throughout the catalogues. What's more, examples of *Lekanomanteia*, that is, basin divination, *Nekromanteia*, divination through a human skull, Seeing People Long Dead, *Hygromanteia*, (water bowl divination), and Causing Visions all have plentiful examples within both the PGM and *Leyden Papyrus*.

In four of the seven Planetary Hours described, we find permutations of Saturn and the Moon, and given the nature of the Moon as the Gateway of the Dead, this should give some idea of the landscape in which these Spirits reside. It also bears mentioning that this theme or coherence of the Moon and Saturn which has been explored at length in this text is best exemplified by these particular Hours and their Spirits. This is further underscored by the offices appearing to be sequentially structured save the office of Causing Visions, which should presumably be completed first, otherwise we must initially have the ability to communicate with Demons before we can work divination with them through a basin, just as we must first have the ability to communicate with the Dead before we can perform Hygromanteia.

---

98 Which may have arrived into Byzantium via the cultural influence of the Bogomils, an eleventh to sixteenh century Gnostic Christian heresy which thrived during the First Bulgarian Empire immediately north of Byzantium.

While other days may be best for the creation of talismans or for other types of magic being performed to change one's lot via the medium of the Spirits, these Seven Hours in particular rule over the practice of Divination more specifically, a fundamental skill in the art of practical magic. Both the techniques of talisman creation and divination possess consistencies with what is described in modern parlance as *Evocation*, while these fourteen Spirits in particular appear to be quite specifically Guardians or Tutelaries which rule over temporal access points that enable the sorcerer to develop the requisite skills and abilities to communicate with both Demons and the Dead. Working in these Hours, then, to both conjure Spirits as well as create talismans which aid us in these pursuits, alongside sessions in which we sit in communication with them to learn and refine our methodologies, is highly recommended. Dream incubation is another technique which can be of immense practical use in this regard, it is a perfectly Lunar form of divination and one which is highly attested throughout history. Of course, if the sorcerer is already in possession of a suitable lamen it should most definitely be used in such experiments, as should an appropriate Circle and the Knife. Exploring these Hours and learning from the Spirits which reside within them should be our initial goal when attempting to begin work with this magical text. There are other Hours on Saturday which should also be considered tutelary, specifically the third and sixth Hours of the Day, and the fourth, seventh, and eleventh Hours of the Night.

PART VI: THE INSTRUCTION

✠

APOTROPAIA

While three manuscripts of *Hygromanteia* possesses details of a complex Lamen or protective talisman known as the *ourania*, which Marathakis suggests is a shortened version of the phrase *ourania sphragis*, or 'heavenly seal', none of them possess complete details which can be feasibly replicated in the modern day. From what instructions remain, we find the medium of *unborn calf parchment* to be an essentially impossible item to acquire. Many examples exist throughout the grimoire tradition and so the sorcerer may already possess a Lamen used in other forms of magical endeavour. If so, I would simply suggest that one continues to use this as your primary phylactery and means for compelling Spirits. If however, the sorcerer would enjoy creating a new item then instructions are found in PGM IV. 2785-2890 form a suitable alternative. The instructions are brief, potent, and well attested.

In all cases every tool and medium shall have been consecrated prior to this event. Now prepare for yourself some natron. This is done by creating a fifty-fifty mixture of baking soda and salt in an oven-suitable dish. Then add consecrated water to the mixture to create a thick, runny paste. Put this in the oven at a high temperature and keep watch over it until the water evaporates. You will have a dish full of hard, brittle crystals which you should then grind into a fine powder with a pestle and mortar. The natron powder should then be sealed in an airtight container.

Take a lodestone, preferably a flat-surfaced magnetic disk, and either etch the following image upon its surface if you have the skill, or pen the image onto consecrated virgin parchment or paper with a specifically-created ink. The image is of the three-faced Hekate. The central face shall be that of a young woman wearing horns, the left shall be that of a dog, and the right shall be the face of a goat. If this is done on parchment it should then be attached to the loadstone with a natural bonding agent such as a mixture of flour, salt, and water. The natural glue should be allowed to dry before the entire object is cleaned with natron and a little consecrated water.

The final instruction of the spell is to then drop the charm into the blood of someone who has died a violent death, then make food offerings to it while saying the spell which precedes these instructions found in lines 2785-2870[99] known as the 'Prayer to Selene for any Spell'. This is understandably difficult to accomplish, and so an alternative becomes a necessity. We are to find the grave of someone who has died before their time, preferably at your local graveyard and, with the greatest care and respect, take a spoon's worth of soil. This soil should be *bought* from the grave with offerings being made firstly to the Guardian of the Graveyard who stands at its threshold, as well as to the inhabitant of the grave from which you take the soil. A suitable offering to the Guardian is a coin pushed into the earth or between the stones near the entrance, as well as a libation of wine. Flowers, fresh spring water, milk, and wine are suitable for the departed. In all cases, divination and permission are necessary from both Guardian and the Spirit of the deceased, and under no circumstances should any gravesite be modified or desecrated in any way. This should be done with reverence, dignity, and great humility.

Once this soil has been bought and returned home it can be mixed with small drops of consecrated spring water and ground into a thick mud while repeating these words adapted from PGM VII. 643-51 over it seven times:

> You are dirt; you are not dirt but the head of Athena. You are dirt; you are not dirt, but the guts of Osiris, the guts of IAŌ PAKERBĒTH SEMESILAM ŌŌŌ Ē PATACHNA IAAA. ABLANATHANALBA AKRAMMACHAMAREI[100] EEE, who has been stationed over necessity, IAKOUB IA IAŌ SABAŌTH ADŌNAX ABRASAX
> At this hour come to my aid and protection[101]

---

99 Betz, pp 90-92.

100 Compare with PGM III. 494-611, the Name of the third Hour of Helios (Betz, p. 31). Gershom G. Scholem, in *Jewish Gnosticism, Merkabah Mysticism, and Talmudic Tradition*, (New York: The Jewish Theological Seminary of America, 1965), notes that "Akrammachamarei (written with a double M) also reached Coptic Gnostic literature and, in the Pistis Sophia [...], makes its appearance as the name of the first among the αόρατοι, Θεοί, a divine Triad standing high in its Gnostic hierarchy of deities. Standing at a somewhat lower station, Akrammachamarei, as master and ruler of the heavenly firmament, is called upon in one of the curse tablets published by Audollent." (Scholem, p. 96).

101 Betz, p. 136.

An Alternative Rubric for the Harvesting of Materia

While the *Hygromanteia* possesses a great deal of materia magicae what it lacks is a solid example of how to properly harvest such things and as a result we find ourselves once more looking to PGM IV. 2967-3006 to find a suitable method. The specific importance of why this spell was chosen will become clear in time, but for now understand that it maintains a thematic coherence with the material presented in this text concerning the mysteries of the North.

Once more the sorcerer should have natron to hand, some pine tree resin, as well as some Egyptian temple incense known as *kyphi* or *kaput*. Instructions for creating this wonderful incense can be found easily. As well as the Egyptian source which was recorded on the walls of the temple at Philae, the recipe was also included in the work of Dioscorides, Plutarch, and Aelius Galenus, although each has a somewhat different interpretation of the necessary ingredients. Alternatively frankincense, which has a long history with ritual purity and used extensively throughout western religion and magic, may be used as an incense.

Begin with the necessary ritual purifications and cleaning, followed by the sprinkling of natron over the materia to be harvested. Carry the burning pine tree resin around the location three times. This incense is then placed down safely and allowed to fumigate the materia. The *kyphi* or frankincense is then burned and a libation of milk is given to the soil. As you make the following prayer, harvest the plant while invoking the Name of the daimon (God) to whom the herb or plant is being dedicated. This calling will aid in establishing the necessary virtues of the materia, making it effective for its intended purpose. The following is to be said as the harvesting occurs:

> You were sown by Kronos,[102] you were conceived by Hera, you were maintained by Ammon, you were given birth by Isis, you were nourished by Zeus the God of rain, you were given growth by Helios and dew. You are the dew of all the Gods, you are the heart of Hermes, you are the seed of the primordial Gods, you are the eye of Helios, you are the light of Selene, you are the zeal

---

102 Compare with the Bear Spell (page 114) and the origin myth of Typhon.

of Osiris, you are the beauty and glory of Ouranos, you are the soul of Osiris' daimon which revels in every place, you are the Spirit of Ammon.

As you have exalted Osiris, so exalt yourself, and rise just as Helios rises each day. Your size is equal to the zenith of Helios, your roots come from the depths, but your powers are in the heart of Hermes, your fibres are the bones of Mnevis,[103] and your flowers are the eye of Horus, your seed is Pan's seed. I am washing you in resin as I also wash the Gods[104] even as I do this for my own health. You shall also be cleaned by prayer and grant us power of Ares and Athena. I am Hermes. I am acquiring you with Good Fortune and Good Daimon both at a propitious Hour and on a propitious day that is effective for all things.[105]

Once this is said the sorcerer takes the materia and places it upon pure linen which is then rolled or folded accordingly. Then seven seeds of wheat and seven seeds of barley, mixed together with honey, are placed where the roots of the materia lay.

✠

An Opening Rite

The following is adapted heavily from PGM XIII. 734-1077,[106] a spell which was originally designed to produce a vision through a child-seer. Being armed with a list of the Names of the Gods of the Days and Hours, as well as the twelve rulers of the Months, with the seven-letter Name which has been written in the *Key*.[107] This is the Name which 'brings alive all your books'.[108] What is learned after the

---

103 The Holy Bull of Heliopolis, the incarnation of the Sun God Prē. See Betz, p.95.

104 Betz, p. 95. The reference is to the daily temple cult and care for the divine statues, including their washing, dressing, and feeding.

105 Adapted from Betz, p. 95.

106 Betz, pp 189-95.

107 *The Key of Moses*, apparently a book that belonged to the author of these texts in the PGM. See Betz, p. 172-73.

108 Betz, p. 189.

performance of this ritual is to be kept secret, "for in it there is the Name of the Lord, which is Ogdoas,[109] the God who commands and directs all things",[110] under whom all the Spirits of creation have been subjected. Therefore, learn and conceal, for without this God's intervention nothing will be accomplished.

Bathed and dressed in fresh linen, enter your Circle and approach the East at Dawn on the day of your work. A consecrated lamen should be worn and the Circle should be cut with a knife. Incenses such as frankincense and mace should be burned with prayers spoken. Water should be cast to the quarters, calling upon a suitable Spirit such as Elelogap. All materia needed should have been prepared earlier and placed upon the altar. Fire is a necessity, and should also be consecrated. If the sorcerer has established their Spirit court, then the Names of their Intermediary should be called alongside those Spirits of the quarters that may take their seats at the quarters.

Come to me, you from the four Winds, ruler of all, who breathed Spirit into mankind for life, and the hidden and unspeakable Name which cannot be uttered by human mouth, at whose Name even the Daimons, when hearing, are terrified, whose is the Sun,
ARNEBOUAT BOLLOCH BARBARICH B BAALSAMĒN PTIDAIOY ARNEBOUAT,
and the Moon, **ARSENPENPRŌOUTH BARBARAIŌNE OSRAR MEMPSECHEI**

They are unwearied eyes shining in the pupils of mankind, of whom heaven is head, ether body, earth feet, and the environment water, the Agathos Daimon. You are the ocean, begetter of good things and feeder of the entire World. Yours is the eternal processional way in which your seven-lettered name is established for the harmony of the seven sounds of the Planets which utter their voices according to the twenty-eight forms of the Moon,

SAR APHARA APHARA I ABRAARM ARAPHA ABRAACH PERTAŌMĒCH AKMĒCH IAŌ OYE Ē IAŌ OYE EIOY AEŌ EĒOY IAŌ

---

109 The Ogdoad (The Eightfold) refers to the eight primordial Gods worshipped in the city of Hermopolis.
110 Betz, pp 189-90.

Yours are the beneficent effluxes of the Stars, Daimons and Fortunes and Fates, by whom is given wealth, good old age, good children, good luck, a good burial. And you, lord of life, King of the heavens and the Earth and all things living in them, you whose justice is not turned aside, you whose glorious Name the Muses sing, you whom the Eight Guards attend,

Ē Ō CHŌ CHOUCH NOUN NAUNI AMOUN AMAUNI

You who have truth that never lies. Your Name and your Spirit rest upon the good. Come into my mind and my understanding for all the time of my life and accomplish for me all the desires of my soul.

For you are I, and I, you. Whatever I say must happen, for I have your Name as a unique phylactery in my heart, and no flesh, although moved, will overpower me; no Spirit will stand against me, neither Daimon nor visitation nor any other being of Hades, because of your Name, which I have in my soul and invoke. Be with me always for good, a good God dwelling on a good wo(man), yourself immune to magic, giving me health no magic can harm, well-being, prosperity, glory, victory, power and desirability. Restrain the evil eyes of all those that would oppose me, but give me charm in everything I do.

ANOCH AIEPHE SAKTIETĒ BIBIOU BIBIOU SPHĒ SPHE NOUSI NOUSI SEĒE SEĒE SIETHŌ SIETHŌ OUN CHOUNTIAI SEMBI IMENOUAI BAINPHNOUN PHNOUTH TOUCHAR SOUCHAR SABACHAR

I am of the god **IEOU ION EON THŌTHO OUTHRO THRŌRESE ERIŌPŌ IYĒ AĒ IAŌAI AEĒIOYŌ AEĒIOYŌ ĒOCH MANEBI CHYCHIŌ ALARAŌ KOL KOL KAATŌEN KOLKANTHŌ BALALACH ABLALACH OTHERCHENTHE BOULŌCH BOULŌCH OSERCHNTHE MENTHEI**,

for I have received the power of <u>Abraham</u>, <u>Isaac</u>, and <u>Jacob</u>,[111] and of the great God, Daimon,
IAŌ ABLANATHANALBA SIABRATHILAŌ LAMPSTĒR IĒI ŌŌ,
God.

---

111 Feel free to adapt these three Names to any other set of patriarchs or matriarchs that have relevance to your personal practice.

Part VI: The Instruction

Aid me to accomplish my goals, Lord,
PERTAŌMECH CHACHMĒCH IAŌ OYĒE IAŌ OYĒE IEOU AĒŌ EĒOY IAŌ

Before the rising Sun, stretch out your right hand to the left, doing the same with your left hand, say "A" to the North, putting forward only your right fist, say "E" to the West, extending both hands in front of you, say "Ē" to the South, holding both on your stomach, say, "I". Return to face the East and, touching the ends of your toes while facing the Earth, say "O" Looking to the Air above the Sun, having your right hand on your heart, say, "Y" Looking into the Sky directly above, having both hands on your head, say "Ō".

I call on you, eternal and unbegotten, who are one, who alone hold together the whole creation of all things, whom none understands, whom the gods worship, whose Name not even the gods can utter. Inspire from your exhalation, ruler of the pole, him who is under you; accomplish for me _____.

I call on you as by the voice of the male Gods,
IĒŌ OYE ŌĒI YE AŌ EI OY AOĒ OYĒ EŌA YĒI ŌEA OĒŌ IEOU AŌ
I call on you, as by the voice of the female gods,
IAĒ EŌO IOY EĒI ŌA EĒ IĒ AI YO ĒIAY EŌO OYĒE IAŌ ŌAI EOYĒ YŌĒI IŌA

[Looking toward East]
I call on you, as the winds call you. I call on you, as the dawn.
A EE ĒĒĒ IIII OOOOO YYYYY ŌŌŌŌŌŌŌ

[Looking to the South]
I call on you as the South.
I OO YYY ŌŌŌŌ AAAAA EEEEEE ĒĒĒĒĒĒĒ
I call on you as the West.
Ē II OOO YYYY ŌŌŌŌŌ AAAAAA EEEEEEE

I call on you as the North.
Ō AA EEE ĒĒĒĒ IIIII OOOOOO YYYYYYY

I call on you as the Earth.
E ĒĒ III OOOO YYYY ŌŌŌŌŌ AAAAAAA

[Looking into the sky]
I call on you as the Sky.
Y ŌŌ AAA EEEE ĒĒĒĒĒ IIIII OOOOOOO

[Looking directly above]
I call on you as the Cosmos.
O YY ŌŌŌ AAAA EEEEE ĒĒĒĒĒ IIIIII

Accomplish for me _____ , quickly. I call on your Name, the greatest among Gods. If I say it completely the Earth and mountains will shake, the Sun will stop amid the Heavens, the Moon shall be stricken with terror, the sea, the rivers, and every liquid will be petrified, the whirling stars of the cosmos will be thrown into confusion. I call on you,

IYEYO ŌAEĒ IAŌ AEĒ AI EĒ AĒ IOYŌ EYĒ IEOU AĒŌ ĒI ŌĒI IAĒ IŌOYĒ AYĒ YĒA IŌ IŌAI ŌĒ EE OY IŌ IAŌ, the Great Name.
Become for me Lynx, Eagle, Snake, Phoenix, Life, Power, Necessity, Images of God,

AIŌ IŌY IAŌ ĒIŌ AA OYI AAAA E IY IŌ ŌE IAŌ AI AŌĒ OYEŌ AIEĒ IOYE YEIA EIŌ ĒII YY EE ĒĒ ŌĀOĒ CHECHAMPSIMM CHANGALAS EEIOY IEEA ŌOEOE ZŌIŌIER ŌMYRYROMROMOS

[If necessary repeat again from AIŌ and add the final sequence]
Ē II YY ĒĒ OAOĒ

✠
A Ritual to Selene

FIG.5: SELENE.

After three days of quiet contemplation and fasting, awaken before first light and bathe, donning fresh clothes before entering your ritual space. Frankincense should be burned as incense before any other. Kneel while facing the East at dawn. Recite the Astrachios or the Lord's Prayer three times and then the Hail Mary. Give honour, glory, and thanks to the Divine, and pray with a warm and fervent heart for what you want to accomplish. Inflame yourself into awe. Turn to the Planet, and upon seeing it, recite its Prayer. Do this first before you Conjure the Spirits of the Hour. This Conjuration shall begin with the Names of the Angels and Demons of the first Hour of Day and the first Hour of Night, for they possess the highest authority and shall move the Spirits into action, their Names possessing much power and virtue. With this accomplished, you shall begin to make your image or talisman, perform divination, cast your spell, or make further conjurations.

The Incense and Ink of the Moon

For the incense, find and mix equal parts of saffron, bay root, the upper parts of peony, and blackberry root. If bay root is not available, then take the upper parts of the caper bush[112] and daffodil root. Dry and grind this mixture into a fine powder and mix with white beeswax.[113] This is then dropped onto the coals as you create your image or perform your operation to the Moon. The ink of the Moon is made from saffron, musk, rosewater, and a drop of your own blood.[114] This potent ink may be written upon the hide of a rabbit[115] and should be fumigated with styrax and galbanum.[116] The following conjuration may then be spoken during the fumigation because they are very useful for making the Spirits obey.

Prayer to the Moon

Lord and Master, the ruler of the living and the dead, who fashioned man in your wisdom, in order to dominate your creatures with piety and prudence, assist me, your servant, so that I may receive the grace to subdue the Planet Moon and complete the operation I have started. I conjure you, Moon, most beautiful purple of heaven and consolation of the night. I conjure you by your orbit, by your renewal, by the innumerable degrees you pass through and in your following Names:

BALIADĒ, ONITZĒR, SPARONĒ, SŌRTĒRKHA, GABĒD, OUTOUPŌN, KEOULĒS, GŌMEDĒM, KAPHIBAN

By these Names I conjure you, Moon, grant your grace and your virtue to my rite.

---

112 Capparis spinosa, the caper bush, also called Flinders Rose.

113 White beeswax can be bought as granules fairly easily.

114 These ingredients can be ground up, mixed, and left to steep before being added to an ink medium.

115 This may be used, if one has access to such things. Parchment cut into the shape of a rabbit which has had rabbit hairs added is an excellent alternative.

116 Ferula gummosa. See the Ketoret in the Book of Exodus 30.34.

The Conjuration of the Hours

I conjure you, Messengers of the First Hours of the Day of the Moon, **GABRIEL** and you, **ARESIEL**, and by your virtue and authority I call upon the Demons of the First Hours of the Day, come now forth **MAMONAS**, and you **NYKTIDON**, come now forth in fair and peaceful form, bearing no harm or ill will unto me (or my companions), that you, great Spirits, who have been appointed for the provision and service of Mankind, move and compel NN. and NN., Spirits of the (first) Hour of the Day/Night, being the Hour of (Planet), to come eagerly unto this Circle, with kindly strength and compassion, for I conjure you by your God, who ordered you to stand as Guardian over this Hour. – (Burn the incense)

The Image of the Moon

When the Sun is in Cancer, together with the Moon, at the hour of the Moon, take pure silver, and make an image in the likeness of a woman. Have her holding a distaff and spin.[117] Trace on her forehead these Names with the knife of the art: SIOLEM, LODAR, IAKHŌ. And on her chest: EKPAGMOS. And on her right hand: SKABOIMION. And on her left: OGLYDŌN. Then, fumigate her with styrax and galbanum.[118] Finally, hide her under the threshold of your workshop or your house, and you will sell whatever you want.

The Conjuration of the Moon

Lord Almighty, supreme, creator of all, king of kings, who fashioned man, who adorned heavens with stars and the Earth with flowers, before the sight of whose power every creature, visible or invisible, trembles, I, your unworthy servant, beg you and entreat you to hear me and subdue to me this planet of the Moon, its powers and its virtues. Lady Luna, the order and the knowledge of the world, the purple of the sky, the consolation of the night, and the Queen of the constrained spirits; Lady Luna, the indication of time, the sign of all celebrations, and festivals, I conjure you, by the high throne of God, by your shining rays, and by the

---

117 Distaff: A stick or spindle on to which wool or flax is wound for spinning.
118 Galbanum (Ferula gummosa): A medicinal herb or resin from Iran, Turkey, and the Mediterranean.

resurrection of God, obey me. I conjure you by the Cherubim and the Seraphim, by all the orders of the angels and in the following names by all the orders of the angels, and in the following names:

GALABĒR, BENOĒL, AGRAKOĒL, ADEMAEL, THIELAPHOĒL, AREPHIEL, ZOGOTHOUL, HYGALAĒL

Show your grace, your power, and your virtue in this operation. Amen.

☦

The First Spirits of Day and Night

Marathakis and Greenfield detail a variety of Short Lists describing highly truncated and simplified versions of each Planetary catalogue. While these lists struggle to agree on which Names belong where, and it is likely the Long Lists are much later historically, we can examine the details spread out across the various manuscripts and find just enough information to propose an attempted reinterpretation of this rather murky layer of the Hierarchy of Time. *Hierarchy* is probably not the correct word or even manner by which we should be approaching this material and so, while maintaining consistency of technique, we propose a new approach.

As mentioned above in the Instructions for working with the Moon, we see that the original description found in A details the conjuration of four Names under the aegis of Saturn, namely the Angels Sakatiel and Ktenoel, and the Demons Aledephor and Kledator. An equivalent for Ktenoel cannot be found in the Angelic catalogue of Saturday, which leaves it in an unusual position. What's more, both Aledephor and Kledator inhabit the same position: ruling the first Hour of the Day, with Aledephor appearing in A and B, while Klendator is found in G and M. H lists the ambiguous Eliditor. There is the chance both of these Names are in fact the same Name which has been divided and later interpreted as distinct from one another, a process that is very common in Spirit catalogues. We also find certain rulers of the Planets, such as the Demon of the Moon *Tartaroēl*, having seemingly minor positions astrologically speaking within the Long List, replaced by the Demon, Kakiston.

In the examples given in the Instruction we find that two Spirits are mentioned for both Angelic and Demonic forces. This modus operandi was preserved; however, instead of presenting yet more Names as 'Superiors' to the Long Lists below, the Names used were kept internal and without any apparent top-down bias. Thus, to begin any rite to a given Planetary Day and Hour we shall begin by Calling upon the Angel and Demon of the first Hours of both Day and Night for the Day on which we are performing our operation.

The 1st Spirits of Day and Night		
Day	**Angelic Rulers**	**Demonic Rulers**
Moon	Gabriel / Aresiel	Mamonas / Nyktidon
Mars	Samouel / Gorfil	Kakiston / Aprox
Mercury	Ouriel / Hydroel	Loutzipher / Taxiphon
Jupiter	Raphael / Sitioel	Meltiphron / Asmodas
Venus	Agathouel / Talkidonios	Goulion / Stragiton
Saturn	Sakatiel / Arniel	Klendator / Tekhar
Sun	Mikhael / Opsiel	Asmodai / Hoistos

The following is extracted from MS Mediolanensis H2 infer. as an example of the Names of the Spirits which rule over the Days. No two of these short lists agree, with the number of Spirits assigned per Planet, spelling, and positioning all highly variable. It is shown here for the sake of example.

Day	Angel Rulers	Demon Rulers
Moon	Gauriēl, Sagiēl, Khariēl Elphēloem, Dōniēl, Perdikēm, Sēnēl	Ortanoēl[119]
Mars	Ouriēl, Sabatiēl	Berouēl
Mercury	Mantatoēl, Spekouēl, Apodekiēl	Khabēl, Sēnouanēl
Jupiter	Sepepheēl, Raphaēl	Ponitos Pilatos[120], Ornēel
Venus	Anaēl, Kyrsoēl	Bateb, Baltasar, Prōtizēkati
Saturn	Ktētoēl	Berzebouēl
Sun	Mikhaēl, Oureēl,[121] Phēlouēl, Sabēel, Doniēl	Khthoniēl, Oriamēl, Opithounianos

---

119 Usually Tartarouēl.
120 Pontius Pilate.
121 A duplicate of the third demon of Jupiter.

Part VII: The Gods of Time

✠

Images, Prayers, and Conjurations

The following Prayers and Conjurations have been largely adapted from MSS Petropolitanus Academicus, Atheniensis 125, Monacensis Gr. 70 and Gennadianus 45, and with reference to the translations of Ioannis Marathakis. It should be noted that while the presentation here is nominally Christian, this should in no means limit our work to such a perspective. The Names of the Greek Gods have been reintroduced and in the case of Saturn the translation of *Abyss* is alternatively given as *Hades*. The sorcerer should approach these Prayers and Conjurations as a blueprint for their personal work and make suitable adaptations where necessary. Personalise the prayers and have fun experimenting. The Spirits themselves may even give you hints and clues as to how to accomplish this.

The Names which are described in the Images are to be traced with the knife as opposed to being physically written. This is best done while vocalising the Names themselves and with an appropriate incense burning, which is then used to fumigate the image. These images need not necessarily be made on the specified metal, although they certainly pack a punch when they do. Parchment, or even virgin (i.e. unrecycled and never touched) paper, if also consecrated before use, is just as potent. If an item made of the specified metal is present this can help, especially if a sympathetic Spirit has been conjured previously alongside the item and been gifted it as a home. This Spirit can be conjured during the ritual to grant its virtue to the image without the image itself being specifically made of the metal in question.

The Image of the Moon

When the Sun is in Cancer, together with the Moon, at the hour of the Moon, take pure silver, and make an image in the likeness of a woman. Have her holding a distaff and spin. Trace on her forehead these Names with the knife of the art: SIOLEM, LODAR, IAKHŌ. And on her chest: EKPAGMOS. And on her right hand: SKABOIMION. And on her left: OGLYDŌN. Then, fumigate her with styrax and galbanum. Finally, hide her under the threshold of your workshop or your house, and you will sell whatever you want.

The Prayer of the Moon

Lord, and master, the ruler of the Living and the Dead, who fashioned man in your wisdom, in order to dominate your creatures with piety and prudence, assist me, your prophet, so that I may receive the grace to subdue the Planet Moon and finish the operation I have started. I conjure you, Selene, most beautiful purple of the heaven and consolation of the night. I conjure you by your orbit, by your renewal, by the innumerable degrees you pass through and in your following Names:

BALIADĒ, ONITZĒR, SPARONĒ, SŌRTĒRKHA, GABĒD, OUTOUPŌN, KEOULĒS, GŌMEDĒM, KAPHIBAN

In the above Names I conjure you, Selene, grant your grace and your virtue to the operation I attempt.

The Conjuration of the Moon

Lord Almighty, supreme, creator of all, king of kings and Lord of Lords, who created, and fashioned man, who adorned the heaven, with the stars and the Earth with flowers and animals, before the sight of whose power every creature, visible or invisible, shivers and trembles, I, your unworthy servant, beg you and entreat you to hear me and subdue to me the virtues of the Moon, its powers and its virtues. Lady Luna, the order and the knowledge of the world, the figure of heaven, the consolation of the night and the Queen of the constrained Spirits; Lady Luna, the indication of time, the sign of all celebrations, and festivals, I conjure you, Luna, by the high throne of God, by the Solar rays, by the rest of God, by the Cherubim and the Seraphim, by all the orders of the holy angels, and in the following Names:

KHARIŌMŌ, GALLAGIL, BENOUĒL, AGRAMOUĒL, ADEKAĒL, THYELOĒL, RHAPHAEL, ZYGOTHOEL, GALAĒL

For your above names, do not disobey me, but grant your grace, power and virtue in the work I am going to attempt.

The Image of Mars

In his Hour and with the Sun in Aries and the Moon in Scorpio make the image of a young man holding a sword on iron. The following Names are to be written upon his forehead: KAMADŌN, RHARA, PISALĒ, and SAMOUĒL, and the Name ARSAKAĒL upon his hand. Fumigate with a drop of your own blood. If you carry this with you at night or in war it shall serve you well.

The Prayer of Mars

Eternal God, dreadful God, indescribable God, whom no man can see, whom the abysses saw and bristled and the living became lifeless, grant us your grace in order to be able to subdue the Planet Mars. I conjure you, fiery Mars, O great warrior, by God who created the fiery virtues, the intellectual natures and the whole fiery host. I conjure you by your virtues, by your orbit, by your brightness and in your following Names I conjure you by your virtues, by your orbit, by your brightness and in your following Names:

OUTAP, NOUĒT, KHOIBI, GAINIAK, AKHLĒ, IMPYRA, NOLIEL, SIAT, ADYKHĒL, TZANAS, PLĒSYM

Grant me your grace towards the purpose I am working for.

The Conjuration of Mars

Oh Lord, powerful and mighty, whose anger dries the bottom of the sea, whose powerful glance breaks mountains, the mountains feared you and the abyss was terrified by you. You whom every Choir of archangels and angels worships. In your Name, Lord, and in the greatness of your kingdom, I, your servant, dare to attempt every work. O bellicose Mars, by the heart of the mighty lion, and by the flame of the strong, burning fire, to obey me. I conjure you, Mars, sanguine and daring, by the air, by the earth and by the centre of the earth, to obey me. O Ares, who rejoices in the death of men and grieves in happiness, O you of calamity, I conjure you by Him, whom you and every stellar essence in creation fears, and in your following fiery Names:

AGLA, ASĒR, PIORIRŌTH, ALBAND, ĒNDŌR, OMĒR, SKONAPHOR, KALONOS, ALMANOS

In your above Names, grant your grace and your virtue to my present work.

The Image of Mercury

In His Hour with the Sun in Gemini and the Moon in Leo or Virgo, make an image in the likeness of a judge (magister) holding a book in his right hand upon cast copper. Trace these Names upon his forehead: GERGIEL, MANDYSIK, GAINER, GENERMA, MŌYSĒS;[122] upon his chest, KHOUSINOGLISI, OUBNOKHLĒ, YSĒ, and on his right hand, RHITĒS and KOLPĒS. Fumigate this image with the skin of a hare and with frankincense. If you wish to learn any art or skill, then place this image under your pillow and He will come to you in your dreams and teach you. You will learn quickly and not forget.

The Prayer of Mercury

Almighty Lord, the inventor of wisdom and knowledge, the maker of heaven, omnispective and omnipotent, grant us the grace you bestowed upon your Planet Mercury, so that we may swiftly accomplish our goals. I conjure you, most wise and all-knowing, most erudite, most intelligent, adaptable, most watchful Mercury, by your foresight, by your orbit and virtue, and in the following Names:

NYPHAN, PIOUT, NOMĒN, SELAK, NIAR, MEREPŌN, STEMĒNOS, PYRIPTON, MIET

In your above Names I conjure you; grant your grace and your virtue to the operation I wish to attempt.

The Conjuration of Mercury

In the Name of the all-benevolent God, who dwells on high and beholds the humble, who searches the reins and hearts, the Lord of Spirits, the king of Heaven and Earth, grant your grace, O Lord, that I may subject the powers of the Planet Mercury. O Mercury, the most skilled in logical arguments, of unfathomable wisdom in every science; who divides and

---

122 Marathakis, p. 260.

distributes the art of each person; since without you all things, mobile or mobile, cannot be known; O Hermes, greatest philosopher and orator, and ruler of minds; I conjure you by the one who created you and placed you in the heavens. I conjure you by your heaven, by your sphere, by the treasure and by the secret wisdom of God, by His strong and immeasurable hand and by all the myriads of angels, do not disobey me. I conjure you in the following Names:

SIBORAZ, HYIELISPHAK, IAGROU, HYSOREŌNŌ, EILILŌPH, NAENDŌR, GELSTAMŌT, KHASELŌN, ASEOULOUĒL, TERATOUŌN, SPHALIKON, KYRMAĒN, BARNIDŌN

In your above Names, grant me your grace and your virtue, in order that any work I attempt to be effective and true; by the omnipotent of God, Amen.

The Image of Jupiter

In the hour of Jupiter with the Sun in Sagittarius and the Moon in Pisces, make the image of a young man on tin. In his right hand he holds a twig and bears these Names upon his chest, made with the knife: KHAMETIĒR, PHARŌKH, and MESELĒTH, and the Name PARAPARA upon his hand. Fumigate this image with myrrh and carry it with you for luck in every affair.

The Prayer of Jupiter

O Lord God, the creator of all things, visible and invisible, King of kings, and Lord of lords, give me the grace and power in order to subdue Jupiter, for everything is possible to you, Lord. I conjure you, Jupiter, by your wisdom, by your knowledge, by your curative virtues, by the heavenly orbit you follow, and in your following Names:

ANŌPH, ORSITA, ATNOS, ORIGEN, ATZINIEL, TENNEOSTGE, NIER, RHANITZA,

Grant me your grace.

The Conjuration of Jupiter

Lord, our God, the great, praised and incomprehensible, whose height of divinity is immeasurable, unto you, I pray. I, the unworthy, beg the height of your compassion, hear me and make this attempt and the work I want to do, to be highly effective. I conjure you, most valorous and most beneficial Jupiter, by the immeasurable ankle of God, do not disobey me. I conjure you, O Mighty Zeus, by the grace of all herbs, by your valour and justice, by your miraculous virtues and in your following Names:

MISTHAN, MESAOU, ALASIGNŌ, PELKHAOUS, AABIŌ, KEDESŌD, OLABĒR, SEDIŌ, AŌLŌI, AZANŌR, MERRAN
In your most great and valourous Names, grant your grace and your virtue by the work I am going to do. Amen.

Image of Venus

In Her Hour, with the Sun in Taurus and the Moon in Gemini, make the image of a young woman upon yellow brass holding an apple in her right hand. Trace the following Names upon her forehead: ESAPONA, GRAMME, PITIGIE, EDITRE; upon her heart trace the Name, ELIGŌN, and upon her hand, GOURIRETH. Fumigate Her image with mastic and labdanum.[123] Carrying this image upon your person will inspire the love of anyone whom you desire and be favoured by all women.

The Prayer of Venus

Eternal God, you of infinite benevolence, who wards away all evil by your great philanthropy, who infinitely possesses the inscrutable sea of goodness, from whom derives the compassion of love, I beg your gentle kindness, grant us the full virtue of the Planet Venus, in order that I may accomplish my desires. I conjure you, most beautiful one, by your grace, by your orbit, by your virtue, by your sweetness and in your following Names:

---

123 Labdanum, otherwise known as Ladanum or Ladan. Obtained from Rockrose, either Cistus ladanifer in the western Mediterranean or Cistus creticus in the east. This incense has biblical origins.

ERETH, LABAK, SIAR, SATĒR, TOUID, TOUIMAR, RHESPHODŌM, SYRŌPH, KAKYM, SENTIAP

I conjure you in your Names; do not disobey me, but assist me by your grace in my present work.

The Conjuration of Venus

In the name of the supreme God, in His most desirable Name, I conjure you, most harmonious, most beautiful and most fair lady Venus, who lies in valour and in the might of love, who tortures the human flesh from within. O Venus, who rules over passion and distributes love, most comely Venus, who leads every yearning in the hearts of men and women and moves the entrails of people; O lady, crowned with the wreath of love, I beseech for your power, in order to torture the people I want and make them fall under my feet. I conjure you, Aphrodite, by the one who created you and placed you in heaven. I conjure you by the seal that is in your heart ♀, by your wreath, by your heaven, and in your following Names:

MONTOARAN, MAUGORAN, KTIOËL, PYRGETON, LIOIKON, IKARIZI, IAKŌR, LADOKON, PARINOS, PHREKTIOUZ, PHALOUMPOL, KRAIPOPHŌN, ALLĒOPŌN, ESTOGE, IASĒPH, ZAGLYTAI, KRIGENOS, ŌOULAN

In your above Names, do not disobey me, but grant your grace and your virtue in the work I am going to attempt.

The Image of Saturn

In the Hour of Saturn with the Sun in Capricorn and the Moon in Aquarius, neither being ill-affected by either Malefic, the sorcerer shall make the image of a white haired old man with the finger of his right hand pointing to the ground. The following Names are to be written upon his forehead using the knife of the art: GORAL, KĒON, EKPERIKOUPH. On the right hand, OUELGAĒR. This image is to be fumigated with sulphur.[124] Bury this image for a single night in a place in which you believe something has been hidden. The following night retrieve the image and place it under your pillow. The following night return once more to the place you believe something has been hidden and bury it in the same place once more. Return again the following night and you shall see a light over it, 'like a taper'. Mark this place and you shall not fail.

The Prayer of Saturn

Eternal God, irresistible might, who arranges everything towards our salvation; grant me the grace to subdue the planet Saturn to my will. I conjure you, Saturn, by your orbit, by your air, by your properties, by your heaven, by your brightness, by your virtue and in your following Names,

GASIAL, GOKYSAEL, EKTASER, BELTOKHIEL, ENTATZIK, Grant me the grace, virtue, and power during the Hour of your rule.

The Conjuration of Saturn

Lord our God, the great and supreme, who created and fashioned mankind, the abyss (Hades) saw you and feared, the living saw you and became lifeless. In His Name and by His great and mighty power, I conjure you, fearsome Saturn, by the heights of the Heavens and by the depths of the Sea, by your pre-eminence and antiquity, I conjure you, Saturn, you who have dominion over all the kingdoms of the world, do not disobey me, but come, swiftly, swiftly and without delay. O cold

---

124 Sulphur is a very common incense to be attributed to Saturn and sometimes Mars. It is, however, fantastically dangerous. Elsewhere in *Hygromanteia* we find the Head of a snake is suggested for Saturn as well as pepper. *Picatrix* also offers some rather grizzly materia for incense of Saturn such as monkey blood, bird brains, or the guts of a black cat; however, it does also suggest dates, juniper, myrrh, saffron, myrtle or olive leaves, and mandrake seeds, though the root of mandrake is also popular in other grimoires. The *Book of Oberon* suggests frankincense, which is highly generic but appealing to almost all aerial Spirits. Other options that are more specifically Saturnian would be hemlock juice or henbane seeds which are also found in *Oberon*. Various Keys of Solomon suggest Magnetite, which should never be used under any condition; while they also recommend pine wood or resin or black poppy seeds, which are far easier to use. The PGM suggests storax liquid and *Sepher Raziel* suggests costus. For more, consult Rankine's *The Grimoire Encyclopaedia*.

and distant Lord Kronos, who holds authority over every harm, who gives treasure and who offers everything. I conjure you in your following Names:

ARPHIN, ORKIP, OULIOB, BERIK, OURAPHON, SARŌK, TAIMON, ODEL, SIGĒP, SOTAD

Grant your grace and your virtue to every work I want to accomplish.

The Image of the Sun

In his Hour, with the Sun in Leo alongside the Moon, create the image of a man crowned with gold with a sceptre in his right hand. Trace these Names upon his chest with the knife: AMPRASĒS, AMPRAS, PANTALON, and on his right hand, APATAIŌN. Fumigate this image with nutmeg. If this image is carried upon your person, you shall have anything you need from those in authority, as well as love.

The Prayer of the Sun

King of kings, and Lord of lords, supreme essence, eternal power, incomprehensible and infinite light, the most generous dispenser of mercy, look upon us with your grace and benevolence, so that we will be able to subdue this Planet, the Sun, and possess its virtues. I conjure you, untouched, unconquered Sun who shines at day, by your annual cycle, by your wings, by your virtues and in your following Names:

GLIBIŌTH, ANTIKON, LĒTHETIOUD, AGLIPAL, ELBAOUKH, PYPOUR, NOPLIOSĒM, OOGĒN, GODASOST, TOULTOURAPH, IŌNAN

In these Names I conjure you; do not disobey me, but assist my present work by your grace.

The Conjuration of the Sun

In the Name of the Almighty and supreme God, I conjure you Lord Sun, the illuminator, the king of all stars, the begetter of vision. O Sun, who nurtures and causes the herbs and the trees to bear fruit, who adorns the whole world with majesty, who banishes adversities in the darkness, and who divides the beautiful things from the ugly ones;

O Sun, the embellishment of the priceless things, the beauty and the majesty of pearls, gold and precious stones, the glory of the kings and the thought of the judges; I conjure you, Sun, Lord Sun, inconceivable, incomprehensible, who sees the powers of heaven and understands the splendours of the supreme God. I conjure you, Lord Helios, O candle that burns before the dreadful God SABAOTH, do not disobey me. I conjure you in the following Names:

PITHANKOUZ, DORIEL, SINAE, MADOËL, LYTROPHAR, PHRYKTOUEL, PELKADŌN, ANDRAPHOR, IYMEDŌN, ALIANOS, GARAROUĒL

In your above Names, grant your grace, power and virtue in the present work I want to attempt.

✠

Address to Aion

An alternative preliminary conjuration is given here, that being PGM IV. 1167-1226, 'Stele useful for all things, even delivering from Death. Do not investigate its contents,' translated by W. C. Grese. This stele is a conjuration addressed to the primordial God of Time, Aion, who emerged from Chaos and set about creating the Universe. He is a complex deity with many links to other pantheons which existed in the melting pot era of Hellenic Egypt, with connections to Phanes, Dionysus, Osiris, Plutonius, and the syncretic Greco-Egyptian God Serapis. He is perhaps best known in his Mithraic *leonto-cephaline* or lion-headed form, winged and encircled by a serpent. Aion is often depicted alongside snakes, particularly the Ouroboros, which represents the belt of the Zodiac and the cyclic nature of Time. For our purposes, Aion is called upon in his cosmogonic form to initiate our sorceries, reforming the Universe by conjuring something of this most powerful and enigmatic deity to be present alongside us as we work.

Part VII: The Gods of Time

I praise you, the one and blessed of the eons and father of the world, with cosmic prayers. Come to me, you who filled the whole universe with air, who hung up the fire from the [heavenly] water and separated the earth from the water. Pay attention, form, spirit, earth and sea, to a word from the one who is wise concerning divine Necessity, and accept my words as fiery darts, because I am a [(wo)man], the most beautiful creature of the god in heaven, made out of spirit, dew, and earth.

Heaven, be opened; accept my words.

Listen, Helios, father of the world; I call upon you with your name

AŌ EY ĒOI AIOĒ YEŌA OUORZARA LAMANTHATHRĒ KANTHIOPER GARPSARTHĒ MENLARDAPA KENTHĒR DRYOMEN THRANDRĒTHRĒ IABE ZELANTHI BER ZATHRĒ ZAKENTI BIOLLITHRĒ AĒŌ OYŌ ĒŌ OŌ RAMIATHA AĒŌ ŌYŌ OYŌ ŌAYŌ:

the only one having the original element. You are the holy and powerful name considered sacred by all the angels; protect me, NN, from every excess of power and from every violent act. Yes, do this, lord, god of gods,

IALDAZAŌ BLATHAM MACHŌR PHRIX AĒ KEŌPH EĒA DYMEŌ PHERPHRITHŌ IACHTHŌ PSYCHEŌ PHIRITHMEŌ RŌSEROTH THAMASTRAPHATI RIMPSAŌCH IALTHE MEACHI ARBATHANŌPS,

creator of the world, creator of the universe, Lord, God of gods, MARMARIŌ IAŌ. I have spoken of your unsurpassable glory, you who created [Gods, Spirits, and Lords of Time]. The ten thousands of angels stood by [you] and exalted the heaven, and the lord witnessed to your Wisdom, which is Aion,

IEOYĒŌĒ IAĒAIĒŌĒYOEI,

and said that you are as strong as he is. I invoke your hundred-lettered name which extends from the sky to the depth of the earth; save me, for you are always ever rejoicing in saving those who are yours,

**ATHĒZE PHŌI AAA DAIAGTHI THĒOBIS PHIATH
THAMBRAMI ABRAŌTH CHTHOLCHIL THOE OELCHŌTH
THIOŌĒMCH CHOOMCH SAĒSI ISACHCHOĒ IEROUTHRA
OOOOO AIŌAI**

I call upon you, the one on the gold leaf, before whom the unquenchable lamp continually burns, the great god, the one who shone on the whole world and [radiant over the Kingdom of Man], lord,

**IAŌ AIĒ IŌĒ ŌIĒ ŌIĒ IĒ AIŌAI AI OYŌ AŌĒ ĒEI IEŌ ĒYŌ
AĒI AŌ AŌA AEĒI YŌ EIĒ AEŌ IEY AEĒ IAIA IAŌ EY AEY IAĒ
EI AAA III ĒĒĒ IŌ IŌĒ IAŌ**,

for a blessing, lord.[125]

☩

A Spell of the Bear which Accomplishes Anything

The following spell, adapted from PGM IV. 1331-89,[126] may be used as a means to summon Typhon, utilising his authority as a means to experience dreams, for divining using a lamp, or for the conjuring of Spirits or Gods. The presumed modality is one of a cosmogenic intervention from the Gods who are summoned by necessity to restore the Primordial Chaotic forces unleashed by the Titan. It should be compared with *Leyden Papyrus* Col. V, which begins by instructing us to, "stamp on the ground with your foot seven times and recite these charms to the Foreleg [Ursa Major], turning to the North seven times."[127] Much as the Dragon that resides in the Ninth Heaven presented above from Marathakis' translation of MS Atheniensis 1265, Set-Typhon is addressed as being a "form of soul that resteth above in the heaven of heavens,"[128] as well as, "O god who is above heaven,"[129] perhaps alluding to its nature being above the realm of the fixed Stars. Marathakis also makes the note

---

125 Betz, p. 61.
126 Betz, pp 63-64.
127 Griffith & Thompson, p. 45.
128 Griffith & Thompson, p. 47.
129 Griffith & Thompson, p. 47.

that the original author presumed this realm above the Fixed Stars was connected to Saturn.[130]

It is generally known that Typhon is the child of Gaea and Tartarus; however, in an alternative and far more interesting telling of the myth[131] it is Kronos, the Father of Time, who sires Typhon at the request of Hera[132] by anointing two eggs[133] with his semen which she then buries within the Earth.[134] The Bear Spell which follows appears to derive from this specific myth as its initial historiola describes it in detail. We find then, that this modality engages with mythic narrative and so the sorcerer is advised to explore the writings of the pre-Socratics to explore more of this fascinating subject.

While the following rite of conjuration and vision can be accomplished without the need for any of the materia described below save the sorcerer's usual tools, they are highly recommended for its first performance. All of the proposed ingredients save Ethiopian cumin and the admittedly ambiguous although efficacious Egyptian walking onion are very difficult to acquire. Thankfully, as we have already seen, we have a methodology which can be utilised to help in such situations.

---

130 "The Head and Tail of the Dragon are in fact the points where the orbit of the Moon intersects the Ecliptic. However the author of this section believes that it is a celestial body placed above the eighth heaven of the fixed stars, according to the geocentric system, and that its orbit is somehow connected with Saturn." (Marathakis, p. 255).

131 G. S. Kirk, J. E. Raven & M. Schofield, *The Presocratic Philosophers: A Critical History with a Selection of Texts*, second edition, (Cambridge: Cambridge University Press, 1957).

132 "They say that Ge [Gaea] in annoyance at the slaughter of the Giants slandered Zeus to Hera, and that Hera went off and told Kronos about this. He gave her two eggs, smearing them with his own semen, and telling her to store them underground: from them, he said, a daimon would be produced who would displace Zeus from power. And she in her anger put them under Arimon in Cilicia. But when Typhon had been produced, Hera had become reconciled to Zeus, and revealed everything; and Zeus blasted Typhon and named the mountain Aetna." Kirk, Raven, & Schofield, p. 58, translating from Homer's *Iliad*.

133 Possibly the twin Pole Stars Kochab (Beta Ursae Minoris) and Pherkad (Gamma Ursae Minoris), having overthrown the Pole Star of Thuban.

134 This bears a striking similarity to the historiola which appears in the abovementioned Harvesting Spell adapted from PGM IV 2967-3006, "You were sown by Kronos, you were conceived by Hera", "you are the seed of the primordial Gods", as well as the use of seven seeds of wheat and barley.

Using the abovementioned spell from PGM IV. 643-51 (See above, Part VI) take some lard and consecrate it with spring water to wash it clean. Divide it into three equal parts. Replace the word *Wine* or *Dirt* with, *fat of a black ass, fat of a dappled she-goat*, and *fat of a black bull*. Perform three separate passes of this rite, one for each part of lard. With this accomplished take some Ethiopian cumin and mix it with all three pieces of lard. This shall be your offering to the Bear, the stars of Ursa Major. Repeat the above process with hairs taken from a four-legged carnivorous beast and replace the appropriate word with *Bear*. Create a plaited cord by means of your art into a headband or diadem. This shall be your phylactery. Acquire storax resin and grind it into a very fine powder and add it to a base of olive oil. Do this with similar consecrations and purifications of Water. Create this mixture when the Moon is well-aspected and waxing.

Take the fat and apply it to your lips so that the Voice may be possessed of the materia that you may better call upon Set-Typhon. Apply the storax oil to your body, your forehead, the nape and back of your neck, shoulders, chest, back, navel, groin, arms, legs, and feet. During your first petition you should hold in your hand a single shoot of an Egyptian walking onion. If possible, you should also prepare for yourself a piece of rope made from date palm fibre which can be made into a belt. Alternatively, acquire another form of natural rope and perform the above ritual which first cleanses the materia and then brings upon it a new virtue. After first locating the constellation of Ursa Major in the heavens, proceed to speak the following formula:

> I call upon you, holy, very powerful, glorious, and strong autochthones, assistants of the great God and the powerful chief Daimons, you who are inhabitants of Chaos, of Erebos, of the Abyss, of the depth, of Earth, you who dwell in the recesses of Heaven and lurk in the hidden places of houses, shrouded in dark clouds, watchers of things not to be seen, Guardians of Secrets, Leaders of those in the Underworld, Administrators of the Infinite who wield great power over Earth, earth-shakers, foundation-layers, Servants in the chasm, terrifying fighters, fearful Ministers, you who turn the spindle and bring freezing snow and rain, traversers of the air, causing summer heat, wind-bringers, Lords of Fate, inhabitants of dark Erebos, bringers of compulsion who send flames of fire, who bring snow and dew, wind-releasers, disturbers of the deep, treaders on the calm sea, mighty in courage, grievers of the heart, powerful Potentates, cliff-walkers, adverse Daimons, iron-hearted,

wild-tempered, unruly, Guardians of Tartaros, misleading Fate,
all-seeing, all-hearing, all-subjecting, Heaven-walkers, Heaven-shakers,
Spirit-givers, living simply, who gladden the heart, you who join together
Death, revealers of angels, punishers of mortals, sunless revealers, rulers
of Daimons, almighty, holy and unconquerable!

AŌTH ABAOTH BASYM ISAK SABAŌTH IAŌ IAKŌP MANARA SKORTOURI MORTROUM EPHRALA THREERSA;

Come now, swiftly, swiftly, and without delay, peaceably and affably to
attend to my rite and complete for me (the goal of our Work).

Once completed, write with consecrated myrrh ink on a piece of virgin
papyrus, parchment or paper the hundred-lettered name of Typhon.
Make this in the shape of a Star and bind it in the middle of the core
with the following letters of the Name. Once completed repeat the
Name seven times.

ACHCHŌR ACHCHŌR ACHACHACHPTOUMI CHACHCHŌ CHARACHŌCH CHAPTOUMĒ CHŌRA CHŌCH APTOUMIMĒ CHŌCHAPTOU CHARACHPTOU CHACHCHŌ CHARA CHŌCH PTENACHŌCHEOU.

Comparative Bear Spells

PGM IV. 1275–1322, LINES 1275-1289

I call upon you, the greatest power in heaven (***others***: "in the Bear") appointed by the lord god to turn with a strong hand the holy pole NIKAROPLEX Listen to me, Helios, Phre; hear the holy [prayer], you who hold together the universe and bring to life the whole world [...].[135]

PGM IV. 1275-1322, LINES 1301-1307

Alternatively:
THŌZOPITHĒ, Bear, greatest goddess, ruling heaven, reigning over the pole of the stars, highest, beautiful-shining goddess, incorruptible element, composite of the all, all-illuminating, bond of the universe, AEĒIOYŌ [...], you who stand on the Pole, you whom the lord god

---

135 Betz, pp 62-63.

appointed to turn the holy pole with a strong hand: THŌZOPITHĒ.[136]

PGM IV. 1323-30

KOMPHTHO KOMASITH KOMNOUN[137] you who shook and shake the world, you who have swallowed the ever-living serpent and daily raise the disk of the sun and of the moon, you whose name is ITHIOŌ EI ARBATHIAŌ Ē, send up to me, NN, at night the daimon of this night to reveal to me concerning the NN thing.[138]

PGM VII. 686-702

"Bear, Bear, you who rule the heaven, the stars, and the whole world; you who make the axis turn and control the whole cosmic system by force and compulsion; I appeal to you, imploring and supplicating that you may do the NN thing, because I call upon you with your holy names at which your deity rejoices, names which you are not able to ignore.

BRIMŌ, earth-breaker, chief huntress, BAUBŌ [...] [shooter] of deer, AMAM[AMAR]APHROU [...], universal queen, queen of wishes, AMAMA, well-bedded, Dardanian, all seeing, night-running, man-attacker, man-subduer, man-summoner, man-conqueror, LICHRISSA PHAESSA, O aerial one, O strong one [O Goddess of Erymna - Preisendanz translation], O song and dance, guard, spy, delight, delicate, protector, adamant, adamantine, O Damnameneia, BREXERIKANDARA, most high, Taurian [Bull-like, the Bull is a consistent symbol associated with the spells of the Pole Star], unutterable, fire-bodied, light-giving, sharply armed. Do [the requested goal of the operation]" (Add the usual).[139]

PGM LXXII. 1-36.
This is adapted for clarity from the original translation by W. C. Grese.

Rite concerning the Bear:

Prepare an earthen censer. During the sixth Hour of the Night offer to the Bear moss of a savin[140] in it. Do it before three days after you called on the Bear nine times from a high roof. Write on a piece of papyrus with a

---

136 Betz, p. 63.

137 According to F. Ll. Griffith, 'The Old Coptic magical texts of Paris,' *Zeitschrift für Ägyptische Sprache und Altertumskinde*. 38 (1900), 85-93 (p. 93), this may be Coptic for 'Earth-shaker, Ground-shaker, Abyss-shaker'.

138 Betz, p. 63.

139 Betz, pp 137-38.

140 The meaning of this word is uncertain.

mixture of ink and myrrh concerning everything which you want, add the Name, **NEBOUTOSOUALĒTH**, and show both the strip of papyrus and what is written on it to the Goddess [...] within one hour. Speak with your hands folded on your head, praying in a loud voice to the Bear:

"Hail, O Queen of mortals and of Gods. Hail, heavenly ruler, Queen of Men. Depart [...] I beseech you [...]."[141]

---

141 Betz, p. 298.

Appendix: Satanael

Le diable garde les lieux inferieurs, ils'etait fait Satan quand ilavait fui du ciel, car son nom etait Satanael.

Some aspects of the dualism found in the *Magical Treatise* may have arrived into Byzantium via the cultural influence of the Bogomils, an eleventh-century CE Gnostic Christian heresy founded during the First Bulgarian Empire in and around modern day North Macedonia, Serbia, Romania, and Bulgaria. The Spirit Satanael, the eighth Angel of Night on Wednesday, is a central figure and counterpart of Jesus Christ within the Bogomil account of creation. There are two variations organised into two families of manuscripts, the South-Slavic and the Russian, which are known as the extra-canonical Biblical text III Baruch.[142] A similar account to this myth is found in 2 Enoch.[143] The cosmogonic account found in these texts diverges significantly from the Genesis story we are familiar with and may be a survival of a radically different competing variant of the myth.

The Greek Apocalypse of Baruch, written between the 1st and 3rd centuries of the common era by either a Jew or Christian, is an eschatological account of a spiritual journey, a descent, in which Baruch alongside a guiding spirit, witnesses the various realms of the afterlife. Orlov states, "Despite the availability of the Greek evidence, scholars noted that in some parts of the pseudepigraphon the Slavonic text seems to preserve more original material."[144] He goes on to say that, "Harry Gaylord's newly assembled Slavonic sources show several areas where Slavonic appears to be closer to the original. One of such areas concerns the fourth chapter of the text. Gaylord observes that the overall structure and content of Chapter 4 in Slavonic seems closer to the original than the extant Greek version,[145] which in this part, "has suffered the most at the hands of Christian scribes."[146]

---

142 Gaylord, 'How Satanael lost his "el"', p. 304.

143 Still considered canon in Ethiopia.

144 Andrei A. Orlov, *Azazael and Satanael in Early Jewish Demonology* (Albany: SUNY Press, 2011) p. 114.

145 The original of which has been lost.

146 Orlov, p.114.

Appendix: Satanael

The Slavonic account which was central to the heresy of the Bogomils describes *Satanael*, Prince of the Grigori,[147] as the creator of the universe and mankind after his fall from Heaven after the creation of the Stars by the Demiurge on the fourth Day.[148] He is then granted seven ages to hold dominion over the world, giving the commandments to Moses, founding the Christian Church and ultimately leading mankind astray. The cosmogonic themes of a stellar revolution in the heavens, coupled with specific division of seven, places this mythic narrative squarely within the concepts explored within this text and deserves our attention. To quote from III Baruch,

> And he said to Michael, 'Sound the trumpet for the angels to assemble and bow down to the work of my hands which I made.' And the angel Michael sounded the trumpet, and all the angels assembled, and all bowed down to Adam order by order. But Satanael did not bow down and said, 'To mud and dirt I will never bow down.' And he said, 'I will establish my throne above the clouds and I will be like the highest.' Because of that, God cast him and his angels from his face just as the prophet said, 'These withdrew from his face, all who hate God and the glory of God.' And God commanded an angel to guard Paradise. And they ascended in order to bow down to God. Then having gone, Satanael found the serpent and he made himself into a worm. And he said to the serpent, 'Open (your mouth), consume me into your belly.' And he went through the fence into Paradise, wanting to deceive Eve. But because of that one I was cast out from the glory of God. And the serpent ate him and went into Paradise and found Eve and said, What did God command you to eat from the food of Paradise? And Eve said, 'From every tree

---

147 The Watchers.

148 Gaylord notes, "The Palaea tradition is based on the observation that the passage concerns a star and therefore places it on the fourth day of Creation. However, it is not entirely clear from this text if Lucifer is a star or an angel or both. II Enoch interprets the central figure as a dissenting deity, or, monotheistically, the overreaching angel, and places the incident on the second day, when the angels were created. Is it possible that the appearance of Is. 14 in the account of Satan's refusal to worship Adam in the original Penitence of Adam is a fossilized remnant revealing that this is an adaptation of the earlier story, namely that of the revolt of the angels in heaven against God before the creation of Adam?" (Gaylord, p. 309).

of Paradise we eat; from this tree God commanded us not to eat.' And having heard Satanael said to her, 'God begrudged the way you live lest you be immortal; take and eat and you will see and give it to Adam.' And both ate and the eyes of both were opened and they saw that they were naked.[149]

In this account it is notable to underscore that the Angel with the flaming sword is placed over Paradise as a guardian to prevent Satanael from entering, not to prevent Adam and Eve from returning after their expulsion. The serpent is described as an independent actor, distinct from Satanael, who, as a *worm* enters its mouth. The description of Adam being fashioned from mud and dirt is also of interest as it bears a similarity to the description of Man's creation found in the Qur'an.[150]

To continue I will quote from 4.7-15 of the South-Slavic version of III Baruch[151] which contains a unique account of Genesis described to Baruch by his *angelus interpres* during his katabasis. This account contains a description of the five Angels placed over the Garden before the Fall, the plants they attend to, as well as an account of the Flood myth in which the waters sent by God reach the Garden itself, implying something of its celestial nature.

And the angel said to me "When God made the garden and commanded Michael to gather two hundred thousand and three angels[152] so that they could plant the garden, Michael planted the olive and Gabriel, the apple; Uriel, the nut; Raphael, the melon; and Satanael, the vine. For at first his name in former times was Satanael, and similarly all the angels planted the various trees." And again I Baruch said to the angel, "Lord, show me the tree through which the serpent deceived Eve and Adam." And the angel said to me, "Listen, Baruch. In the first place, the tree was the vine, but secondly, the tree (is) sinful desire which Satanael spread over Eve and Adam, and because of this God has cursed the vine because Satanael had planted it, and by that he deceived

---

149 Gaylord, p. 305.

150 Sura 7.12: "He said: What hindered thee that thou didst not fall prostrate when I bade thee? (Iblis) said: I am better than him. Thou createdst me of fire while him Thou didst create of mud".

151 Belgrade: National Library of Serbia, MS Slav. 466.

152 See The Book of the Watchers (1 Enoch 10.11-15).

the protoplast Adam and Eve." And I Baruch said to the angel, "Lord, if God has cursed the vine and its seed, then how can it be of use now?" And the angel said to me, "Rightly you ask me. When God made the Flood upon the earth, he drowned every firstling, and he destroyed 104 thousand giants, and the water rose above the highest mountains 20 cubits above the mountains, and the water entered into the garden, (and took all that was blooming), bringing out one shoot from the vine as God withdrew the waters. And there was dry land, and Noah went out from the ark and found the vine lying on the ground, and did not recognize it having only heard about it and its form. He thought to himself, saying, "This is truly the vine which Satanael planted in the middle of the garden, by which he deceived Eve and Adam; because of this God cursed it and its seed. So if I plant it, then will God not be angry with me?" And he knelt down on (his) knees and fasted 40 days. Praying and crying, he said, "Lord, if I plant this, what will happen?" And the Lord sent the angel Sarasael; he declared to him, "Rise, Noah, and plant the vine, and alter its name, and change it for the better."

How exactly this Spirit, Satanael, came to be included within the Long Lists of the *Hygromanteia* remains unknown. From the available evidence we can say that III Baruch survived from its original Greek form into the Slavic where it became part of the Bogomil heresy, which survived at least until the fourteenth century before vanishing alongside the fall of the Byzantine Empire at the hands of the Ottomans in 1453.

This highly dualistic sect of late Gnostic Christianity, which rejected many aspects of tenth century Christian dogma and regional cultural norms (even going so far as to deny the symbol of the cross), probably found its origins as a reaction against the oppression of the Byzantine state, making it just as much a political as well as a religious heresy. Unfortunately, most Bogomil literature has since been lost or destroyed by the Church, meaning the majority of our understanding of this fascinating group has to be inferred, parsed out from very limited evidence, or deduced from those who wrote polemics against them. Thankfully, there is increasing interest in this subject in recent years by scholars, meaning more is sure to come to light in the future.

What I think we can say, though, with some conviction, is that heterodoxy and heresy survived into the modern day by entering into magical and esoteric practices of the dominant religion of the time, namely Christianity—secreted away lest they be lost forever, and that over the centuries these collections of forbidden knowledge have formed what we know today as the grimoire tradition. These texts then represent the survival of what could not be erased from history.

BIBLIOGRAPHY

Manuscript Sources

Athens, Gennadius Library, MS Gennadianus 45
Athens, National Library of Athens, MS Atheniensis 1265
Belgrade: National Library of Serbia, MS Slav. 466
Greece, Bernardakēdes Private Library, MS Bernardaceus
London, British Library, MS Harleianus 5596
Milan, Ambrosian Library, MS Mediolanensis H2 infer.
Munich, Bavarian Regional Library, MS Monacensis Gr.70
Mt Athos, Dionysius Monastery, MS Athonicus Dion. 282
Naples, National Library, MS Neapolitanus II C. 33
Paris, Bibliothèque Nationale de France, MS Parisinus Gr. 2419
Rome, Vatican Library, MS Vat. Reg. lat. 1300, fols 45, 61
St Petersburg, Science Academy, MS Petropolitanus Academicus

Published Sources

Agrippa, Heinrich Cornelius. *Three Books of Occult Philosophy*, 3 vols, ed. and trans. by Eric Purdue (Rochester, VT: Inner Traditions, 2022)

Al-Biruni, *The Book of Instructions in the Elements of the Art of Astrology*, trans. by R. Ramsay Wright (London: Luzac, 1934; repr. Bel Air, MD: Astrology Classics, 2006)

Anonymous, *Homeric Hymn to Demeter*, trans. by Gregory Nagy, Harvard Center for Hellenic Studies, 2018 <https://chs.harvard.edu/primary-source/homeric-hymn-to-demeter-sb/> [accessed 28 February 2024]

Atallah, Hashem, trans. & William Kiesel, ed. *Picatrix: Ghayat Al-Hakim: The Goal of the Wise, vol. 1* (Seattle: Ouroboros Press, 2002)

Betz, Hans Dieter, ed. *The Greek Magical Papyri in Translation*, 2nd edition, (Chicago: University of Chicago Press, 1996)

Chardonnens, László Sándor. 'Hemerology in Medieval Europe', *Books of Fate and Popular Culture in Early China: The Daybook Manuscripts of the Warring States, Qin, and Han*, ed. by Donald Harper and Mark Kalinowski (Leiden: Brill, 2017) 373-407

Collier, Mark and Stephen Quirke, eds. *The UCL Lahun Papyri: Religious, Literary, Legal, Mathematical, and Medical* (Oxford: BAR, 2004)

Conybeare, F. C., trans. 'The Testament of Solomon', *Jewish Quarterly Review*, 11 (October 1898), 1-45

Dosoo, Korshi & Markéta Preininger, eds. *Papyri Copticae Magicae: Coptic Magical Texts Volume 1: Formularies*. (Berlin: De Gruyter, 2023)

Fanger, Claire, ed. Invoking Angels: Theurgic Ideas and Practices, Thirteenth to Sisteenth Centuries (University Park: Penn State Press, 2015)

Gaylord, Harry E. '*How Satanael lost his "el"*', *Journal of Jewish Studies*, 33, no. 1-2, (1982) 303-309

Greenfield, Richard P. H. *Traditions of Belief in Late Byzantine Demonology*, (Amsterdam: Hakkert, 1988)

Griffith, F. Ll. 'The Old Coptic magical texts of Paris,' *Zeitschrift für Ägyptische Sprache und Altertumskinde*. 38 (1900), 85-93

Griffith, F. Ll & Herbert Thompson, eds, *The Leyden Papyrus: An Egyptian Magical Book* (London: H. Grevel, 1904; repr. New York: Dover, 1974)

Harms, Daniel, James R. Clark, and Joseph H. Peterson, eds. *The Book of Oberon: A Sourcebook of Elizabethan Magic* (Woodbury: Llewellyn, 2015)

Johnson, Brian. *Naming the Heavens: Orations from the Summa Sacre Magice* (West Yorkshire: Hadean Press, 2022)

Jones, Alexander. 'Astrologers and Their Astronomy', *Oxyrhynchus: A City and its Texts*, ed. by A. K Bowman et. al. (London: The Egypt Exploration Society, 2007) 307-314

Kaplan, Philip G. 'Pytheas of Massalia' in *The Encyclopedia of Ancient History*, ed. by Roger S. Bagnall (Malden: Wiley-Blackwell, 2012)

Kieckhefer, Richard. *Forbidden Rites: A Necromancer's Manual of the Fifteenth Century* (University Park: Penn State Press, 1997)

Kirk, G. S., J. E. Raven & M. Schofield. *The Presocratic Philosophers: A Critical History with a Selection of Texts*, second edition, (Cambridge: Cambridge University Press, 1957).

Legard, Phil and Alexander Cummins, eds. An Excellent Booke of the Arte of Magick (London: Scarlet Imprint, 2020)

Lilly, William. *Christian Astrology, Books 1 & 2*, ed. by David R. Roell (London: Macock, 1647; repr. Bel Air, MD: Astrology Classics, 2005)

Marathakis, Ioannis. *The Magical Treatise of Solomon or Hygromanteia*, (Singapore: Golden Hoard Press, 2011)

Müller, W. Max. *Egyptian Mythology*, (Whitefish: Kessinger Publishing, 2004)

Orlov, Andrei A. *Azazael and Satanael in Early Jewish Demonology* (Albany: SUNY Press, 2011)

Peterson, Joseph H. ed. and trans. *The Lesser Key of Solomon* (York, ME: Weiser Books, 2001)

Peterson, Joseph H. *The Sworn Book of Honorius: Liber Iuratus Honorii*, (Lake Worth: Ibis Press, 2016)

Peterson, Joseph H. *Secrets of Solomon: A Witch's Handbook from the Trial Records of the Venetian Inquisition.* (Kasson: Twilight Grotto Press, 2018)

Peterson, Joseph H. *Elucidation of Necromancy* (Fort Worth: Ibis Press 2021)

Peterson, Joseph H, *Grimorium Verum: A Handbook of Black Magic*, second edition (Rochester, MN: the author, 2023)

Pingree, David, ed. *Dorothei Sidonii Carmen Astrologicum* (Leipzig: De Gruyter, 1976)

Porter, John. *A Book of the Offices of Spirits*, ed. by Frederick Hockley and Colin D. Campbell (1583; repr. York, ME: Teitan Press, 2011)

Pseudo-Agrippa. *The Fourth Book of Occult Philosophy*, ed. by Stephen Skinner, trans. by Robert Turner (Fort Worth: Ibis Press, 2015)

Rankine, David. *The Grimoire Encyclopædia vols. 1 & 2.* (Keighley: Hadean Press, 2023)

Raphael, Edwin. *Raphael's Astronomical Ephemeris* (Harrow: W. Foulsham, annual publication)

Salzman, Michele Renee. *On Roman Time: The Codex-Calendar of 354 and the Rhythms of Urban Life in late Antiquity* (Berkeley: University of California Press, 1990)

Scholem, Gershom G. *Jewish Gnosticism, Merkabah Mysticism, and Talmudic Tradition.* (New York: The Jewish Theological Seminary of America, 1965)

Sparavigna, Amelia. 'The Pleiades: the celestial herd of ancient *timekeepers*', *ArXiv.org>physics* (2008) <arXiv:0810.1592v1>

Szpakowska, Kasia. 'Religion in society: Pharaonic', in. *A Companion to Ancient Egypt, Vol. 1*, ed. by Alan B. Lloyd (Malden: Blackwell, 2010) 507-25

Skinner, Stephen and David Rankine. *The Veritable Key of Solomon* (Singapore: Golden Hoard Press, 2010)

Skinner, Stephen and David Rankine. *The Keys to the Gateway of Magic: Summoning the Solomonic Archangels and Demon Princes* (Singapore: Golden Hoard, 2011)

Stratton-Kent, Jake. *Geosophia: The Argo of Magic*, vol. 1 (London: Scarlet Imprint, 2010)

Stratton-Kent, Jake. *The Testament of Cyprian the Mage* (London: Scarlet Imprint, 2014)

Stratton-Kent, Jake. *Pandæmonium: A Discordant Concordance of Diverse Spirit Catalogues*. (West Yorkshire: Hadean Press, 2016)

Stratton-Kent, Jake. *The True Grimoire*, 2nd ed. (London: Scarlet Imprint, 2023)

Thomann, Johannes. 'From *katarchai* to *ikhtiyārāt*: The Emergence of a New Arabic Document Type Combining Ephemerides and Almanacs', in *Proceedings of the 28th International Congress of Papyrology Barcelona 2016*, ed. by Alberto Nodar, Sofia Torallas Tovar, et. al., (Barcelona: Publications de l'Abadia de Montserrat, 2019) 342-354

Thorndyke, Lynn, ed. *The Sphere of Sacrobosco and its Commentators* (Chicago: University of Chicago Press, 1949)

Torijano, Pablo A. *Solomon the Esoteric King: From King to Magus, Development of a Tradition* (Leiden: Brill, 2002)

Ventris, Michael and John Chadwick. *Documents in Mycenaean Greek*. (Cambridge: Cambridge University Press, 1973)

Weill-Parot, Nicolas and Julien Véronèse, eds and trans. 'Antonio da Montolmo's *De occultis et manifestis* or *Liber intelligentiarum*: An Annotated Critical Edition with English Translation and Introduction', in *Invoking Angels: Theurgic Ideas and Practices, Thirteenth to Sixteenth Centuries*, ed. by Claire Fanger, (University Park: Pennsylvania State University Press, 2012) pp 238-287

Weyer, Johann. *Pseudomonarchia Daemonum*. trans. by Paul Summers Young (Hanover: Black Letter Press, 2023)

INDEX

A

Aquarius 42
Aries 35
Ars Goetia 16, 19, 21
Asmodai. *See* Asmodeus
Asmodeus 15-17, 19
Asphodel 76

B

Bear Spell 114-117
  comparative spells 117-119
Book of Oberon 20, 110

C

Cancer 40
  as Gate of Death 12, 17, 43
Capricorn 12, 16, 17, 23, 28, 39, 41, 43, 44, 72, 109
  as Gate of the Gods 12, 17, 43
Cardinal Signs 19
Commentary On the Sphere 19

D

daimon 6, 25
  Agathos 75
Dangerous Hours 37
Days of the Moon 44-46
decans 6, 16
Dignitaries 35
Draco 11-12, 17, 43

E

Egyn 16, 17, 20
Eighth Book of Moses 14
Enmity 30, 33, 34, 40. *See also* Friendship

F

four rulers of the Directions 5
  Asmodai 5, 16, 19, 76, 86, 101
  Astarōth 5
  Berzeboul 5, 74
  Loutzipher 5, 56, 101
  Winds 6, 9, 93
Friendship 30, 33, 34, 40. *See also* Enmity

G

Gemini 40
Grimorium Verum 19, 20, 21, 26, 75

H

Helios-Mithras 12, 14
Heptameron 3, 19, 20, 71, 75
Hours of the Days 3, 4, 21, 28–29, 34
  compared with four classical Elements 22
  Offices 8, 16, 46, 52
  properties of 37–38
  rulers of 5, 14, 23, 87, 92, 100, 117
    Aerial 21, 22, 23, 24, 30
    Infernal 5, 20, 22
    Subterranean 22
    Terrestrial 22
humours 31

J

Jupiter 36
  Conjuration of 108
  Image of 107
  Prayer of 107

L

Leo 41
Leyden Papyrus 14, 26, 87, 114
Liber Razielis 3
Libra 41

Lord of Time 43

M

magical timing 3
Mars 36
  Conjuration of 105
  Image of 105
  Prayer of 105
Mercury 36
  Conjuration of 106–107
  Image of 106
  Prayer of 106
Mithras Liturgy 9, 12
Moon 36
  Conjuration of 104
  Image of 103–104
  Prayer of 104

N

North Star 9, 10, 12

O

On Occult and Manifest Things 19

P

Picatrix 20, 71, 110, 125
Pisces 42
Planets 10
  aspects 24, 28, 32
  Chaldean order 29
  rulers of 100
  spirits of 27
  virtues of 30-31
Pleiades 11, 127
Pole Star. *See* North Star

S

Sagittarius 41
Saturn 37

Conjuration of 110–111
Image of 109–110
Prayer of 110
Scorpio 23, 29, 32, 40, 41, 44, 105
Stratton-Kent, Jake 6, 12, 16, 26, 28
Summa Sacre Magice 3
Sun 36
Conjuration of 111–112
Image of 111
Prayer of 111

T

Taurus 40
Testament of Solomon 5, 15, 20, 25, 74, 86

U

Underworld 6, 11-12, 76
Ursa Major 10, 11-12, 14-15, 17, 114, 116
Ursa Minor 11, 14-15, 17

V

Venus 37
Conjuration of 109
Image of 108
Prayer of 108–109
Veritable Key of Solomon 3, 4, 20, 21, 78
Via Combusta 29
Virgo 41

W

Wanderers. *See* Planets

www.ingramcontent.com/pod-product-compliance
Lightning Source LLC
Chambersburg PA
CBHW071510150426
43191CB00009B/1477

African Performance Review

Vol. 1 Nos 2&3 2007
Contents

Signifying Systems in Traditional African Theatre Aesthetics:
The *Girinya* Ritual Dance of the Tiv people of Nigeria
Gowon Ama Doki   7

Trauma and the Art of Dramatizing History:
A Study of Soyinka's *Madmen and Specialists*
Osita C. Ezenwanebe   31

Environmental Impact Assessment and the Dramatist:
A Conceptual Study of Esiaba Irobi's *Hangmen Also Die*
Norbert Oyibo Eze   46

Feminist Aesthetics in African Theatre of the Colonial Period
Esiaba Irobi   56

Crossing the *Zaure*:
Theatre for Development and Women's Empowerment in Northern Nigeria
Jumai Ewu   75

Beyond the Yoruba Cosmology:
A Contestation of the Africanness of Wole Soyinka's Submission in *Myth, Literature and the African World*
Emmy Unuja Idegu   99

Through Other Eyes and Voices:
Women in *Koteba* and *Mmonwu* Performances
Osita Okagbue   114

AfTA Noticeboard

K.W. Dexter Lyndersay: An Obituary Tribute
Professor Dapó Adelugba   130

The Search for Definitions:
Critical Perspectives on African Theatre and Performance
(Report of the 1st International Conference of the African Theatre Association (AfTA) held at Goldsmiths, University of London, 30 August-1 September, 2007)
Francis Ndu Anike   139

African Performance Review

- A journal of the African Theatre Association (AfTA)